MW01532269

The Story Of Eight

∞

I tell people if you think you need a new reading, don't call me. That's just you wanting it. But if you feel you need it, that's *them* telling you there are new messages.

That's how I like people coming to me. There's a feeling. You might not want to do it because that involves the brain, but if it's a gut feeling, like, "I don't know why. I just had to," that's *them* guiding you.

Check out our first book

Too Bad You're Going To Hell:
A collection of stories and readings by
Spiritual Medium Theresa Marotta
Written by Heather T. Stone

Scan this image with your phone's camera to order our book.

SCAN ME

Already read it? Leave us a review.

Found a typo? Let Heather know at
heathersoulfulgatherings@gmail.com.

Copyright © 2023 Soulful Gatherings

All rights reserved, including the right to reproduce this book or portions thereof in any form whatsoever. For information address SoulfulGatherings.net or Heather Stone via HeatherSoulfulgatherings@gmail.com.

ISBN: 978-1-7330172-2-0

Cover art and images by Mel Mullahey

Graphic design by Marion Birdsell

First edition.

Printed in the United States of America

The Story Of Eight

∞

Readings by Spiritual Medium
Theresa Marotta
Written by Heather T. Stone

Within the truest definition of the simple word, "dedication", I find that while the meaning of the word is easily understood, the concept of this word goes beyond what the brain can hold on to and comprehend.

I am being guided by the concept of dedication to extend my gratitude, respect, admiration and love to my coauthor, Heather Stone. It was through the most unimaginable grief of losses suffered and the ultimate joy of birthing her warrior princess that she was able to complete her goal of piecing together this latest book so that our readers could enjoy the words written between the covers that prove there is life after passing.

I know your babies are watching over you and guiding Sasha and Giovanni.

♥ ♥ ♥ ♥

Hi again. It's me.

You may remember me from my first book. Or maybe we've met in person. My name is Theresa Marotta. My friends call me Terry. I'm an Intuitive Spiritual Medium. I speak to people who have crossed into the great beyond. While I mostly deal with humans, I've also spoken to angels, demons, God, Jesus, the Virgin Mother, and an occasional animal. I deal with the past and present. All mediums are psychic and can read futures, but I choose not to. I leave that to my good friend Dawn.

Many moons ago, during a dream state, I received a message that would change my world. It wasn't like a regular dream where I can see or interact with whatever I dreamt of. This one began with a heavy energy. But not heavy like grief or sadness; heavy like the sun. I stared at a void. A giant area of divine light. It was just me standing alone - or so I thought, until I felt a familiar presence. Archangel Michael entered from my right side. He always comes in on my right side. Right side means it belongs to me directly because Jesus sits at the right side of the Father.

Now, I've interacted with this archangel many times. Sometimes he gives me messages I need to figure out, but not this time. This time, his message was direct and to the point.

"It's time to write a book," he said.

"What are you talking about? I don't know how to write a book", I argued back. That's me. Standing in front of an archangel, explaining to him he was wrong.

That's when he told me I would not be the one to actually write the book. He said someone else would write it for me and that I already knew who that person was. He said we would write three books together, then this person would continue writing on their own. I was instructed to ask the universe for a sign and my author would show themselves.

A few years ago, I met a woman through work. At the time, I had no idea she was into creative writing. We crossed paths just like we'd done in many lifetimes before. I knew it was time for our adventure to begin again. But you know me. I don't trust anyone alive. I'm from the Bronx. It's in my nature. So instead of reaching out to discuss this with the young woman, I put a sign out into the universe. Back then, my spirit guides were teaching me to be more specific when asking for a sign, so this time I set a date range. If this woman was supposed to be my author, she would contact me in any way, shape, or form within the next three days. Then I waited.

This woman and I were friendly, but we didn't talk all the time. We reached out to each other once every few months to talk about this and that. Usually about a weird dream or event. I enjoyed having someone to talk to about spirits. She was going through her own spiritual awakening and had questions about how to handle it. I helped her whenever she needed me. I hadn't heard from her in a while, but I trusted my spiritual guides and my dad to point me in the right direction. It was five minutes to midnight on the third day. I got an alert that someone posted on my social media. It was her. At this point in her life, she wasn't huge on social media. I don't remember her ever posting anything on my social media before this. I called her right away. As soon as she answered the phone I said, "You had five minutes left".

We published our first book together, Too Bad You're Going To Hell: A collection of stories and readings by Theresa Marotta, written by Heather T.

Stone in 2019. You are currently holding our second book.

I let the spirits guide me when directing Heather on how to write these books. Most of the time, they talk to me when I'm in the shower. Being alone in the water is a type of meditation for me. They send me visions. Then I send her emails. The rest is up to her.

They told me the title for this book. They explained I would meet eight people whose stories needed to be told. They would come to me as clients. Those eight people would write about their readings and the spirits that came through. It would be a way to honor the dead. Why eight? There are several meanings behind that number I wasn't aware of until I did a little research. This is what I learned.

The number eight is a symbol of the balance of justice because it can be divided into two equal parts. The spiritual meaning is infinity, eternality, and limitlessness; a symbol of infinite energy and love. That's what they wanted our second book to be about; infinite energy and love - love that never dies, even when we cross over to the other side. When that happens, we leave our bodies and heavy energy behind, but we never stop loving those who we left behind. That's the meaning behind the number eight and this book.

Our third book will be completely different from what we've done so far. My spirit guides told me to leave this one up to Heather and great things will happen. She hasn't failed me so far, so I'm okay with putting my faith in her. The only hint I will give you is that it's going to be a work of fiction inspired by my readings. Sounds fun, doesn't it?

I've practiced reading people for years, learning as I go. I've even read people during dream state. At first I didn't know I was dreaming. I was simply reading people who were sitting around me on couches. After I finished reading them, they would pat me on the shoulder and tell me I did a good job. Then they explained what other things my signs could have meant. They were teaching me. But then I realized I didn't recognize any of the people. They spoke to me like I knew them, but I didn't recognize them. That's when I figured out not only was I in a dream state, but I was reading the deceased. That's me; always working. Even when I'm sleeping. These days, I barely recognize anyone I dream of. They also set up coincidences in my life, so I know the experience was real. If you've read my first book or ever had a reading from me, you know I believe in life, there is no such thing as coincidence.

The gift comes from a higher being. I call Him God, but call it whatever works for you. Anything that comes from a higher being is three-sided. It's a gift, a blessing, and a curse. It's a cross to bear. I've spent my whole life learning how to use my gift. Sometimes my signs are on point. Sometimes I don't read them right. But that's all part of growing. I used to be able to tell when someone was going to pass away. That's part of the curse. I could smell death on the living, meaning they would cross over soon. I asked God to take away my ability to see death. I didn't want to deal with that part of my "gift" anymore. And He did. I don't see it anymore. I don't smell it anymore. And I'm thankful for that.

When I was young, I saw spirit with my primary eyes. After some practice, I began to see them with my third eye. I've spent decades doing readings by allowing the spirit to take control of my imagination. I allow them to put images or play movies in my head. However, lately I can see them again with my primary vision, which means I know the bad is coming again. People think you can tell the difference between good and evil, but evil is very good at disguising itself - almost to perfection. But that's a story for another book. This one is about the client, the spirits, and me.

My spiritual journey with a client begins well before the client arrives. Let's say you book an appointment with me. Once it's determined you are going to receive a reading, spirits will find me and start relaying messages before the appointment. One lady got in my car a few days before and refused to leave until her daughter finally came in to be read. Some spirits pop in with a brief message. Some break my alarm clock so it shows a certain time that will make sense later during the reading. Crazy things happen when they figure out you're coming to see me.

There are many ways to read people. There are some mediums who use cards. Some use boards, mirrors, glasses of water, or a number of different objects. I do automatic writing. It's a process of producing written words without consciously writing. I allow the spirit to take control of my mind and then I write what they want.

Before I do a reading, I go into prayer. I go into my reading room, light some candles, and begin my protection rituals. I say a few formal prayers I learned growing up Roman Catholic; Our Father and Hail Mary. I say them in honor because I know where my gifts come from. Without them, I can't do this. I need them to help. I ask for guidance and protection during the reading.

Lately, I've been seeing images appear in a poster I have hanging on the wall near my altar. The poster is Christ shown as half man half lion. The images appear like a ghost or spirit would appear through a wall. I see these images with my primary eyes and not my third eye. These images are related to readings I am about to give. Spirit can contact me in so many ways.

I use yellow legal paper to do a reading. I write whatever messages received before the client arrives on this paper in pen. I usually start getting messages during the prayer part. I don't start writing in pencil until the client chooses one out of a box I keep on my table. They pick one out using a gut feeling and rub the pencil in their hands to transfer the energy from them to the pencil. This also helps them concentrate on getting into the headspace needed for the reading to work. They transfer the pencil to me and I start automatic writing with it. It's a way to channel the messages using phrases, words, numbers, or symbols. I jot things down on the paper to be discussed during the reading.

I allow the spirit to give me three important months. Three is my limit. If I allowed more than that, it's more likely I would hit on a month that means something, eventually. Limit what they're allowed to say and the messages get more specific. I'm not cold reading and don't want people to think I am. I write the three months at the bottom of the paper. To me, this means I can use them as the month or corresponding names and numbers related to that month. For example, the month of March could mean the actual month, the number three since March is the third month in the year, the third of any month or the names Joseph, Josephine or Joey since March is Saint Joseph's month. Saint Joseph is the patron saint of moving and houses, so this could also mean someone is moving. Sometimes the spirit tells me to write the month at the top left-hand side of the paper. To me, this means don't use anything corresponding. They are strictly talking about the month.

I make the spirit prove themselves by telling me a memory or current event. And I don't mean one. I make them continue to tell me these types of things throughout the reading.

Some people come to me for more than one reading. Just because I read you before doesn't mean I'll repeat myself. Heck, I probably won't even remember your reading, or the spirits that came through, or in some cases, you. Please don't take offense to this. To receive messages from the spirit world, I need to keep my head clear. I need a clear mind and an attitude without an ego. They can take control of my mind and use it to show me pictures or play movies in my imagination. I'll describe them to you and it's up to you to tell me what it is.

Sounds easy enough, right? Took me years of practice. If you read my first book, you already know how I got here. But this book isn't about me. It's about *them*.

I think it's also important for you to understand that I have a strong New York accent and sometimes when I'm doing a reading, I ramble a bit. When Heather wrote this book, she had a choice to write it grammatically correct or type the readings out verbatim. She chose to keep the readings as real as possible. We have changed very little. She edited out a few things that were a little too personal and made some minor corrections for clarity. Basically, she wrote the way I speak in order to truly capture my personality onto the pages you are about to read.

So, without further ado, I present to you our second book, The Story Of Eight.

Enjoy!

Terry Marotta

Table of Contents

☆ ★ ☆ ★ ☆ ★ ☆ ★

ONE

☆ ★ ☆ ★ ☆ ★ ☆ ★

Losing someone hurts. Sometimes it can hurt so much that we just want to run away from it all and leave our pain behind. Sometimes we try to outrun our anger at the situation. But running away won't work. Eventually, you'll be right back where you started unless you learn to deal with the heartache the best you can. You may just need a sign that your loved one is okay and happy on the other side, but grief can make you blind to the signs all around you. Our loved ones are never far from us, no matter how far and fast we run. So slow down. Take a breath. Smell the roses. Give your heart time to heal. Then take a look around. You'll see the signs, eventually. And if you're still having issues, give me a call. I'm here to help.

☆ ★ ☆ ★ ☆ ★ ☆ ★

∞ The Story of Eight ∞

Linda's Reading

★ ☆ ★ ☆ ★ ☆ ★

Terry: Linda. The pencils are in that box. Please choose one using a gut feeling then I want you to rub it between both hands. It's so funny you picked that one. That's the color of August. I want you to roll the pencil to me. You see, there are already things written down in pen during the first portion of the reading. As I was speaking to you they were giving me signs. They speak to me telepathically. So that means they'll put an image in my mind or play a movie in my head. I heard them say the month of August. That was the first month I had to write. Now it either pertains directly to someone who's passed or someone living to show me the chain of attachment. So when I hear August I can either go to any day in August, the eighth of any month or the number eight. So what's the confirmation for August?

Linda: My father's birthday.

Terry: Okay. Is he still with us?

Linda: No.

Terry: Good. Well, not good. Can I bring him in? I have the energy of a son. Someone's son somewhere. Does this make sense to you? Did you lose a baby? Did you have a miscarriage?

Linda: No.

Terry: Okay, so with Dad's bloodline in mind as this is the only time I will know the bloodline, okay? Did your mom have this miscarriage? It could be an abortion or the baby could have been stillborn.

Linda: My father had a brother that was stillborn.

Terry: There you go. Okay. Perfect. He's with his brother. Is it okay that I bring him in?

Linda: Mm hmm.

Terry: But the brother, he just shows me it's a baby, but now the baby becomes a man because we're all thirty-three on the other side. Does someone carry the brother's name or was someone just mentioning that name?

Linda: I don't know what the brother's name was.

Terry: Okay. I'm just going to leave it there. He makes me feel someone carries this brother's name, so when you find out, and the way you'll find out is not by asking anyone, it's going to coincidentally come across your path. The month of February. What does any day in February or the second of any month or the number two mean to you? Is it someone's birthday? It could be February one through twenty-eight or twenty-nine on a leap year, or the second of any month, or maybe someone has two children?

Linda: It could be a few things. I have two children. My son's hockey number in college is two.

Terry: There you go.

Linda: I was married in February.

Terry: Okay. So Dad knows this. So all he's trying to tell me as we sit down is, "Do you know my daughter has two kids?" He pays particular attention to that grandson who wore the number two. Does that make sense to you?

Linda: That's my older son that's named after his father; my father's father.

Terry: Wouldn't it be funny if the brother was named after him because someone has the name? Oh. I just got the chills. I think that's what it is.

Linda: It could very well likely be.

Terry: Yes. Okay. But he's paying particular attention to that one. Okay? So how old is that one?

Linda: Twenty-nine.

Terry: Oh. The number twenty-nine is archangels. Who's in the medical field?

Linda: My mother's a nurse.

Terry: Okay. And Mom's still with us?

Linda: *Nods*

Terry: Okay. So remember, wait, I didn't tell you this, so how would you remember? If they mention something medically inclined for someone still in body form, then it has a good ending.

Linda: Okay.

Terry: He wants me to tell you the energy in the legs is off for your mom.

Linda: Her ankle has been bothering her.

Terry: Okay. There you go. How does he know this? He visits her. So he knows.

Linda: She wears a brace on it.

Terry: There you go. There you go. "She's slowing down", your father's saying. It's a natural progression. "Don't get nervous", he's saying.

Alright? She's slowing down. The problem is she knows now that she's slowing down, and it's bothering her. It's more of an ego thing, not a fear-based thing, your father's saying. So she may try to overcompensate and that's when she'll hurt herself.

Linda: Exactly on.

Terry: Really? So he knows his wife.

Linda: Exactly. *Laughs*

Terry: Okay. And she'll get frustrated.

Linda: Yes.

Terry: And she might get - his words, not mine - snippy.

Linda: Oh yes. Lately, definitely.

Terry: Okay. Your last month is April.

Linda: That was the birthday of my husband that just passed.

Terry: Okay. Equal male. Equal male means the same generation. Same generation comes in as a husband, boyfriend, brother, brother-in-law, friend or cousin. Are those his clothes?

Linda: Yes.

Terry: That's what he's telling me. They look better on her. But he's saying, "You didn't have to wear those clothes for me to be here. I'm always with you". It was no one's fault, but someone's carrying some kind of guilt. The "what if" or "I should have", "could have", "would have", blah blah blah. So for that, he's sorry. Okay? Both my nostrils - this is going to be weird. Usually, if someone touches my right nostril, that means someone did drugs. Doesn't have to be the way I passed, but I would have had to have done them. The left is drinking. I'm doing both. Both my nostrils are running. I know they are physically not, but they are. Did someone give up drugs and start drinking a little or give up drinking and started with the drugs? Or is someone currently doing both?

Linda: My son is drinking too much.

Terry: Is this the one that your father mentioned earlier?

Linda: *Shakes head*

Terry: This is the other one. Okay. For some reason I'm going to call him - so he says, "Go ahead. I want to see what you call me". He just doesn't like boyfriend, but he wasn't a fiancé.

Linda: We talked about getting married.

Terry: Yeah. So he wants "husband". Is that okay?

Linda: Yeah. That's how I refer to him.

Terry: Okay. Cool. Because he says to me, "I want to see how you refer to me. Because I'm going to tell you right now I don't like "boyfriend" and I wasn't her fiancé". So he is "husband". For some reason, it's your husband who's watching over the one that's doing a little too much drinking. Your father has the first one, the oldest one. He's taking care of that, but that job is not as difficult as what your husband has with the second child. Does that make sense to you?

Linda: Totally.

Terry: Okay.

Linda: They were very close.

Terry: Like a dad? So he was like a dad energy. Okay. He's showing me a beaded bracelet. So is someone wearing a beaded bracelet? Does someone wear one in memory of someone? I feel beads.

Linda: *Pulls something out*

Terry: Oh look at that. What's that?

Linda: It's a string, and I got it after he passed and I always have pearls or beaded bracelets on.

Terry: You know what's funny? The pearls, though, are for April. What was April?

Linda: His birthday?

Terry: That's why. Oh, is that why you wear them? It's his birthstone.

Linda: Well, also he gave them to me and I always wore them. He always gave me pearls.

Terry: That's why. It was his birthstone. April the birthstone is pearls. He's saying not all the same color, though.

Linda: No. He got me black this past Christmas. Black pearls.

Terry: There you go.

Linda: I couldn't wear them all. They're like navy blue, but they're considered black.

Terry: I see you wearing pearls and I said to him, "Can you just make the confirmation a little stronger". And he said, "Yes. They're not all white". Okay. So I want to go to the ones that aren't all white. Were you supposed to get, or maybe one of your children supposed to get either a diploma in something or go back to school? Maybe someone needed to take a test for a new certification or a license.

Linda: My son that we talked about that he watches over needs one more class to finish his degree.

Terry: There you go. He's trying to work on that son to do that. But he's using a lot of excuses, your husband is saying.

Linda: Mm hmm.

Terry: "You know you could wear the ring," he's saying. What does he mean?

Linda: I guess I had a ring at home because we were going to get married. He was still in the hospital and I just got a ring and I was wearing it all the time.

Terry: And why aren't you now?

Linda: I don't know. I don't know. I didn't know if it would be okay with him.

Terry: It is. Oh. I just got the chills. That's why he's saying you could wear the ring. So he already answered that question. You didn't even have to ask it. Because he knows. Of course, wear it. You may have to add a little something to it. Maybe it's plain or something, but absolutely wear that ring.

Linda: It's in the car.

Terry: Oh. Okay. Good. And you're going to wear it on the left finger?

Linda: Yes. I've been wearing it there.

Terry: "That's where you should wear it", he's saying. How long ago did he pass?

Linda: Six and a half months. Almost seven months.

Terry: Oh my God.

Linda: March first.

Terry: That's fine. He doesn't mention March. So again, I don't do psychic readings. Your other month, though, is written up here. September.

Linda: That's my other son's birthday, the older son.

Terry: And he tells me, "Don't go to the nines. Don't do anything, but September."

Linda: His daughter's birthday

Terry: Alright. So he's trying to tell me you have two boys. He has a girl. So far, that's all I know.

Linda: Her birthday just passed.

Terry: Were you doing work near the tub or in the bathroom or were you speaking about doing that?

Linda: *Laughs* I just changed the light fixtures and painted the vanity.

Terry: Okay. He goes, "It's nice". But it proves that he's in the house. They do come to visit us at home, at work, in the car, on vacation and if I said to you your husband's saying he visits you at home, that would be true, but how do you know? See, that's why everything that comes out of their mouth has to be provable. How would YOU know? Well, now I can place him there because he's telling me there was activity going on in the bathroom. Then he gave an opinion. It wasn't a strong positive opinion, by the way. But it's alright, he's saying. It's okay.

Linda: It was just alright.

Terry: Yeah. It was just okay. My head started to hurt me during the prayer part. When my head hurts, remember it doesn't have to be the way someone passed, but I would have had to suffer with it. Do you have an ankle bracelet? He's showing me an ankle bracelet. Who wears the ankle bracelet? Okay. One of your son's. So I know one is eighteen. How old is the other?

Linda: He's twenty-eight. Twenty-nine and twenty-seven.

Terry: Oh. Okay. Do any of their girlfriends wear the ankle bracelet? Because this is what your husband's telling me to tell you. You ready?

Linda: Okay.

Terry: The one who wears the ankle bracelet is going to be a lot of work. Just keep it in the back of your mind.

Linda: The one who wore the ankle bracelet. They broke up.

Terry: There you go. It was a lot of work. There you go. So it makes sense to you. Again, he'll prove everything that he says.

Linda: Yeah. They broke up because she was a lot of work.

Terry: Yeah. Good. Okay. My head started hurting. Remember, it doesn't have to be the way I passed, but I would have had to suffer with it. Did someone have an injury or like alzheimers, dementia, stroke, aneurysm? Anything with the head or the brain.

Linda: Not that I can think of.

Terry: He's going to give me a name. Now if it's not this person's name, they'll give me the name of someone living to show me how they know you. How do you either know the name Nick, Nicky, Nicolas or Nicole?

Linda: That's my son.

Terry: Alright. So this is family then. This is a guy. Pretty tall. Remember, I didn't have to pass from it. Did someone maybe fall off a ladder or hit their head hard? That would be an injury to the head.

Linda: He's had a few concussions.

Terry: Oh. This is your husband?

Linda: My son. Nick. My son. He's the drinker one.

Terry: Oh. So they're really watching over your kids for you.

Linda: He's had a few concussions. He was a hockey player. Got a few concussions. Lost a few teeth.

Terry: Oh. Did he? Okay. You're dreading the fall.

Linda: Yeah.

Terry: Oh. I don't know.

Linda: I guess you can say that. I'm a principal, an assistant principal in the fall with COVID and bussing and school starting.

Terry: Okay. There you go.

Linda: I can say I'm dreading it.

Terry: Okay. So does your husband. Your husband is saying, "She's dreading it". You know you have legal paperwork to sign. So legal paperwork, for me, has to be signed and the signature either has to be notarized or witnessed. It doesn't necessarily mean a lawsuit, okay? Did someone sign a contract of some kind? Did someone buy a new car that has to be witnessed? It's legal paperwork. Were you thinking of moving?

Linda: Just today I had to send all his paperwork in for taxes.

Terry: Those are legal papers.

Linda: I just sent them to the accountant this morning.

Terry: There you go. So he's going to review it. Now, does the accountant sign off on it?

Linda: *Nods*

Terry: Okay. So his signature would be on it. So it's witnessed. Alright. So that's fine. And you did it already?

Linda: This morning.

Terry: There you go.

Linda: Right before.

Terry: That's fine. I felt a sensation in my throat, as if someone had put a tube down my throat. Why would I get that sensation?

Linda: He was intubated.

Terry: Did he have COVID?

Linda: *Nods*

Terry: Oh he did.

Linda: He was intubated in February.

Terry: Oh. There you go. That was the worst of it. He was ready to go at that moment. "I was done. You can't keep a bull down," he's saying. You can't keep a bull down. Now, when they intubate, do they put you in a semi-coma state so you don't feel it? But he felt it. He felt the irritation in his throat. Maybe one of the doctors made a remark. It's so funny about the elephant. I could have given this dose to an elephant. The elephant would have been out. But not him. He was ready.

Linda: He fought it.

Terry: Yeah.

Linda: He fought it.

Terry: Pissed off at the doctors. He was pissed off. They should have just given me a shot to put me out of my misery. He's saying, "You know that doctor Kevorkian. I believe in that. If you know I'm not coming back, why make me suffer?" He goes, "By the way," this is fun for me, "Doctor Kevorkian is on the other side". In the light. Not in the dark because he was an empath, which I didn't know. I have to do research, but anyway I want to thank him for that. He mentions the name Sam. When I hear Sam, how do you know the Sam, Sammy or Samantha? Or, I don't know if it's still even in existence - Sams. There used to be a Costco type of thing.

Linda: No. I never went to Sams.

Terry: No. Alright. So did he know this Sam, Sammy or Samantha?

Linda: He had some racing buddies who were Sam.

Terry: Okay. So he went to visit them.

Linda: Okay.

Terry: The person living - this one's important for the living because I have one passed, but this is for the living person - who's having breast issues is going to be fine. Now, did someone find a lump or was someone told to go to the doctor? Do you have to get tested?

Linda: I've been going and have to go one more time.

Terry: Okay. You'll be fine. Is it with the breast?

Linda: Mm hmm.

Terry: Okay. You'll be fine.

Aha Moment: After the reading Linda said they found a cyst and doctors are monitoring it. Everything is fine.

Linda: I just got the reminder that I didn't go. I was supposed to go back in three months.

Terry: Okay. Because then he makes me feel that someone on the other side had breast cancer or issues.

Linda: She's his ex-wife.

Terry: She passed.

Linda: Yes.

Terry: Okay. He did see her, but I'm not hanging out with her. That's important for you to know, he's saying. "I saw her, but I'm not hanging out." And she's not here. But when someone does this to me, (touches her right breast) that means this particular sign, which would have been breasts in your case, has something to do with both someone on the other side and someone living. You'll be okay. He's handing you the two-dollar bill. Why?

Linda: I once had a two-dollar bill, and I gave it to him and he was so excited about the two-dollar bill and we've kept it. It was in a drawer and it was always there. He said he would buy it. He said, "I'll give you two dollars for that two-dollar bill".

Terry: There you go. Do you still have it?

Linda: Yes.

Terry: Can you keep it in the wallet?

Linda: I can.

Terry: Because he'd rather travel with you than stay at home. Okay?

Linda: Okay.

Terry: Alright. Do you get lightheaded at times? Not dizzy. Lightheaded is different. Like as quickly as it comes - like I'm experiencing it right now - it goes. You don't even have time to sit down. Or it's not as intense that you would have to sit down. One of the physical signs for you that he's around is you'll get lightheaded. It's just a passing wave.

Linda: It happened yesterday at work. I had no idea what was going on.

Terry: Yeah. That's him. He was at work then. Now I can place him there. Sometimes he makes sure you're okay at work. Did he tell you to leave that place? Because he's telling me he doesn't like the energy there. And it doesn't have to do with COVID. It has to do with personalities.

Linda: There are some strong personalities.

Terry: Yeah. There's one in particular.

Linda: Yeah. My secretary.

Terry: Yeah.

Linda: He knows I can't stand her.

Terry. Yeah. That's what he means. So now know that he checks it out. She's keeping files you don't know about. Hold on a second. Not student files.

No. That's not what he's speaking of. She's not doing anything illegal. Okay? But I'm either jotting down, like keeping files. That's what he's saying. I don't know if she's starting a case, or she's going to present a case to you. Something. You may even find a recorder. Just forewarned is forearmed. Speaking of that, who's talking about this tattoo?

Linda: My sons.

Terry: "I shouldn't be the one that says it," he's saying, "but no tattoo." Okay. Let's see what else he has to say. Who's not speaking to who in the family? Was there an argument?

Linda: His niece and his sister are not speaking to each other. It's her mother and her.

Terry: Oh. He knows about this.

Linda: Yeah. They're not speaking.

Terry: He would rather have something planted, he's saying. Was someone thinking of some kind of memorial for him? Like in memory of him, not a service. He's not speaking of a service of any kind, but like in memory of him.

Linda: A scholarship. I always plant stuff in my garden for him.

Terry: For him. That's what he likes because it's life. Now, there may be something that you plant for him, not this season, so you might have planted it already; it's still going to come up next year and it may look like it's dead or dying. Don't get rid of it because what he's going to do is touch that plant or flower, whatever it may be and it's going to come back to life.

Linda: My mother planted a plant for me for him and it looks like it's dying.

Terry: Leave it alone. "Just leave it alone," he's saying. Because you associate that plant like, "No wonder why. Because he's dead". Because you use dead or he died a lot. He passed. He didn't die, he's saying. And you'll see it come back to life. He's back. He's much happier. "Tell her I shaved."

> **Aha Moment**: Sometime after the reading, Linda figured out the plant is a ficus tree her husband had for many years. Sometimes it didn't look like it was in good shape. It's now bigger and stronger than ever and doing well. It's kept in their bedroom and remains there.

Linda: In the hospital he hated it that he couldn't shave. I was there every day, but I shaved him and he hated it. He hated it.

Terry: He's shaved now. Did he hate when you were shaving him?

Linda: No. He just hated having a beard.

Terry: Being grunge.

Linda: Yeah. Being grunge. He hated it.

Terry: Yeah. Because, I don't know, I should do visuals, but I have an ego. I don't need to be seen, but I was doing this. That's why he says, "Tell her I shaved".

Linda: Yeah. He hated the grunge, and he would make me bring in the electric razor to the hospital. I did it a few times.

Terry: Good. But he's nice, clean shaven and good to go.

Linda: Good to go. Good to know.

Terry: He talks. Do you know the name Scott?

Linda: Yes.

Terry: How do we know Scott?

Linda: He's my custodian that drives me up the wall.

Terry: Okay. He thinks he spooked him recently.

Linda: *Laughs* Good.

Terry: But he's saying, "I can't take the credit. It wasn't intentional". So there might be a rumor going around school that there's a ghost in the school because he mentions Scott. I like uncommon names. You see these types of messages, you can't google this stuff. You can't. That's why I like boring messages. We're just having a regular conversation. Because they honestly didn't leave. They left their bodies. Okay. Who has the black toe? Or does someone have a fungus under a nail or discoloration? What's with that?

Linda: I have been running so much that I got that runner's toe.

Terry: Oh.

Linda: On both my feet. I have a black toe on each foot right now - the nail. From running too much.

Terry: The black toe hunny.

Linda: This morning I was going to go for a pedicure. It's just black from running so much.

Terry: "You can't run it out," he's saying.

Linda: All I do now is run.

Terry: Yeah. And you're running away from anger at the situation. He knows you're not mad at him. He's trying to bring someone else in. Who else passed from COVID? I feel mucus coming up my throat.

Linda: I'm thinking.

Terry: Alright. Don't think. Again, he's going to give me a name. If it's not this person's name, it's going to be someone living to show me the chain of attachment. How do you know the name either Jim, Jimmy or James? Was I a patient in the hospital with your husband?

Linda: No. We have friends.

Terry: Okay. Hold on a second. One of those friends involved, did any of them lose someone from COVID because I felt mucus coming up; not staying in my lungs. I'm drowning in mucus.

Linda: His cousin, Richie, passed right before him.

Terry: From COVID?

Linda: It was AIDS and then he got bad pneumonia.

Terry: Okay. Pneumonia is good because that's mucus. Okay. So I'm going to let him come in. Okay? And they're playing cards. Why?

Linda: They were cousins and they grew up doing that.

Terry: Okay. They grew up doing that. I like that. "It's not the scrabble or the word games", he's saying, but he's making fun of scrabble or the word games.

Linda: We played scrabble on his phone every day all day. So that's why I would think he was playing scrabble.

Terry: Nope. He's already telling you no. He's not playing scrabble.

Linda: He played non-stop.

Terry: But he's not doing that now. I think the energy he puts towards playing scrabble is not a positive one. It keeps my mind occupied so I don't have to think about something else. It's something he needed to do, whereas with the cards it's something he wants to do. He puts the letter "Y" here. So when I see just a "Y" do you have an affiliation with either Yonkers or Yorktown?

Linda: I grew up in Yonkers. I lived in Yorktown.

Terry: Okay. There you go. That's all I needed to know. Did they just either fix a street light or was someone just talking about the street light? Did someone get a new street light? Something about a street light. Where do you live right now?

Linda: ██████████

Terry: Oh. Okay. So you do have street lights there. Like on my roads here, at night, we don't.

Linda: I was just talking with someone about how I still run at night in my development because I have street lights everywhere.

Terry: Was one of them out recently?

Linda: I don't know.

Terry: Okay. Look for it next time you run. There's something about a street light. You never know. You may pass one and it may dim and then go out. That just means he's there. It's the street light. When he shows me street lights. I'm just going to assume there are times he goes. "I can't go every time. She's neurotic when she's running. I can't." It's too much for him even though he doesn't have to walk; he can fly during the walk, he's saying. It's too much for him, but he knows you do this. He writes number eighty. Was someone around eighty years old or does 1980 mean something? So that would mean twenty, twenty-one, forty-one.

Aha Moment: After the reading Linda sent me a message.

"There is a streetlight on the corner of the block where we lived that goes on and off that I notice when I am out walking and running. I have also noticed that the streetlights where I run by the water flicker. At times I look up above the streetlights and there is a bird that seems to follow me."

Linda: My mother is turning seventy-nine, so she's almost eighty this month.

Terry: I'm not going to go to her.

Linda: In 1980 I competed in figure skating at the Olympic arena.

Terry: There you go.

Linda: I wasn't in the olympics. Just the trials.

Terry: There you go. That's what he's trying to tell me. Wow! He held his head up high during this whole relationship. "But wouldn't you know it? I was finally happy then this shit happened." Okay. Who's Charles, Charlie, or Chuck?

Linda: My best friend is pregnant right now with a son and she's going to name him Charlie and he's due the week that he passed.

Terry: The son. Someone's having that son. I thought he was on the other side. But he is on the other side, the baby, right now. That's why I don't read pregnant women. The baby goes back and forth - the soul of the baby goes back and forth during pregnancy. But that's what he's saying.

Linda: And she's naming it Charlie and it's due the week he passed.

Terry: There you go. He's asking you not to question if he is alright and he's asking you not to keep asking him to show you signs. He's been showing you the signs. You're just not getting them. They're not going to be in the teacher's mind, meaning logical sense. It will only be in coincidences - what you deem are coincidences. Okay? Please, dear God, tell me you didn't go to a tarot card reader.

Linda: No.

Terry: Who does? Or a Ouija board. Same thing for me.

Linda: One of my kids' friends' wives always reads cards and has asked me if I wanted too and I say no. I haven't done it and I don't want to know.

Terry: Okay. Who had the criminal record? Yeah. You can't go near cards yet.

Linda: His son-in-law had a DWI's kind of criminal record.

Terry: Okay. He's giving you almonds.

Linda: I had almonds - chocolate almonds - yesterday.

Terry: There you go. How does he know?

Linda: And this morning.

Terry: And you didn't even know he was there. Correct?

Linda: Correct.

Terry: He needs you to wear the ring, but not to keep men away from you because that's an attractor to men. It's so you know you're his wife and soul mate, but it was rough in the beginning. What's he talking about? What was rough? Were the conditions not good when you first got together? Did one of the kids give you a hard time?

Linda: His sister gave us a hard time.

Terry: There you go; the roughness he's speaking about, but not anymore. Do you cry in the bathroom?

Linda: All the time.

Terry: Okay. Because he stands outside the bathroom. "And no, you don't need to take time off of work," he's saying. Were you thinking of doing that?

Linda: Just recently I thought about that. I haven't taken any time.

Terry: No. He says, "She'll run. She'll run from here to Connecticut". Now, are you the principal or assistant principal in ███████ schools?

Linda: In ███████ schools.

Terry: Oh in ███████. Do you run near the water?

Linda: All the time in ███████ and in ███████ at the park.

Terry: Okay. The water is very healthy for you. Did you pick something up from the ground to bring home? Was there a certain rock?

Linda: I've never found those rocks that are painted before and since he's passed, I found three. I brought them to the cemetery where he is.

Terry: He's not in the cemetery. He goes there when you're there. You can leave them in your house. This guy has a bit of an ego and I'll tell you why I said that. I'm writing a second book. I did a book already. I choose eight different people to write about as they were before their passing and then parts of the reading. It's called the Story of Eight. He says to me, "I think you should write about me because I'm interesting and then she'll feel a little better about it". Totally up to you. You think about it. I can write about him, how he was as a person before and then the reading follows. Anything personal - it could be to change names - so you have a final say to what's in the chapter devoted just to him if you're interested in it. So I want to make a note. Today is nine-eighteen. I'll send you information. It's up to you.

Linda: He would love that. It's so him.

Terry: Yeah. Because he's been bothering me, saying, "Can't you write about me?" So, as I speak verbally to you, I'm speaking telepathically to them. My granddaughter calls it talking with your mind because she's young. She's only five. She already has the gift. You talk with your mind.

Linda: He always says it was about name recognition. He wanted name recognition.

Terry: Are you kidding me?

Linda: He always said it was about name recognition; getting your name out there.

Terry: Isn't that funny? I don't pay anyone for it. You get a free book, but his name lives on. So it's up to you if you want to use his first name. Whatever you want. I'll send you the information. He's speaking about Colorado.

Linda: I went on a work trip to Colorado.

Terry: When?

Linda: Two or three years ago and I complained that there were no trees where I was in Colorado.

Terry: You're going to hear about Colorado again, but this time you'll be smarter about it, according to him. I don't know. It might be a friend of yours that says, "I was thinking about going to Colorado. What do you think?" The cheesy beads - these are not pearls - the cheesy beads. Do you have beads like from New Orleans? They're cheesy beads. Like from a dollar store. Cheesy beads.

Linda: This is amazing. He had this little T.V. show, and he went out and had the beads on or he would go to the parades in ▮▮▮▮▮ because he was like a politician and always had the beads and the hats. He had them all the time. He had the cheesy beads and hats.

Terry: Oh my God Linda.

Linda: Like the Mardi Gras ones and the Fourth of July..

Terry: Mardi Gras. New Orleans. Those are the ones; cheesy beads.

Linda: The purple and the green.

Terry: He was in politics, right? Did he have different politics than you?

Linda: A little bit. Yeah. He was a republican and I was nothing

Terry: What does that say? *shows paper* Republican.

Linda: He was a district leader - a Republican party chairperson in ███████ and I was just what they call a "non". I was no party. And I would always tell him it was people over party and then that was his slogan.

Terry: Wow.

Linda: Yes. Wow!

Terry: Yeah. It's frigging amazing. So he's telling me, as a favor, so I know something, when he does this about Republicans they're coming back. Republicans are coming back. They should change the name to People Party and that would be a shoe in, he's saying. If they renamed Republican to People's Party, it would be a shoe in. Who's Alex? It could be Al, Allie, Alexander, Alex. Living. Not passed.

Linda: There's a few I can think of.

Terry: Who were you just speaking to or about?

Linda: A guy who wants a job back in my school.

Terry: Okay. He's saying, "You go with your gut feeling with that". Your gut's pretty good when you're not busy being in mourning. Don't feel guilty for having a moment here and there of happiness and laughter. It allows him to stay near you longer. He mentions Holmes, New York - real clear. Do you know where that is?

Linda: I know where it is. I have no idea why he mentions it.

Terry: Good. There will be a nice little connection - coincidentally. "But it won't be a coincidence", he's saying. Now I can ask how you heard about me.

Linda: His daughter. You did a reading for her.

Terry: First name?

Linda: Kristen. It was an online one a few weeks ago.

Terry: Oh. Really? Will you thank her for referring me?

Linda: Most definitely.

Terry: So hopefully it was good.

Linda: Mm hmm. He sent me a ton of messages through her.

Terry: Oh did he?

Linda: So I had to come.

Terry: That's how I like people coming to me. There's a feeling. You might not want to do it because that involves the brain, but if it's a gut feeling, like I don't know why. I just had to, that's *them* guiding you.

Linda: I had to.

Terry: Perfect. This is a spiritual request. Not that I have anything against religion. I don't, but I'm more spiritual. I promised God - whomever that is for you - anyone I read I would ask them when they find themselves totally alone to offer up four very informal prayers. These informal prayers are for four different types of people living. Why? They pray for us because we're close to hell. Hell is starting to seep up. Informal said by the heart is a sentence. Maybe two. So it's for someone living you care about - whatever good wish you want to send their way, someone you don't even know because we have lost souls here or someone you know who is a lost soul, someone you know, but you don't like this person or trust this person. The prayer for that person goes something like, Dear God, please let them find their way. Just keep them away from me. You want to wish them well first, then create the boundary. And for us as a society to stop abusing, torturing and killing kids. I mean, what the hell are we doing? We're demonic - society is. So thank you for trusting me.

Linda: Thank you.

Terry: You feel okay?

∞ The Story of Eight ∞

A Letter From Linda

☆ ★ ☆ ★ ☆ ★ ☆ ★

Anyone who met Bruce immediately would feel respected, valued and special. He was the type of person who connected with people on many levels and would talk to anyone. The first time I met Bruce, I knew he was something special. He was very self-confident, personable, and went out of his way to make friends. Bruce truly was a person and a man with a mission. He loved being a police sergeant, an autocross racer, father, a grandfather, a politician, a husband and a partner. He always brought out the best in people. He could inspire people and without ever telling you what he thought you should do, he would guide you down the path of making the right decisions.

All the people who knew Bruce would agree that he was an extremely strong willed, hard-working, devoted and influential individual who accomplished all that he set out to do. He looked for the good in each person and usually found it. He was always busy – a man in constant motion – but never too busy to share his love of life with those around him.

He was a loving and attentive father and father-in-law, grandpa to three boys (Zack, Tyler and Matthew), brother to Nancy and half-brother to Paul, uncle to Anna and Molly Young, life partner, husband to Linda, step-father to Nick and Robert, colleague, mentor, friend and so much more to all of his people.

Bruce was born on April 1st, 1954. He was born in The Bronx, New York. He had one sister: Nancy and a half brother, Paul. As a young boy, He enjoyed playing baseball and loved the Yankees. He would tell us stories of how he would often watch Roger Maris and Mickey Mantle play in Yankee Stadium growing up.

His sister, Nancy, always told stories of his youth, including how he'd fool his father when he first learned to drive. Bruce's father would let him drive his 1959 Ford Fairlane and, when his father would fall asleep, Bruce would take the car out without permission and visit my mother, Debbie. But somehow, he always managed to park the car in the same spot and his father never found out. Clearly, he always had a love for cars and was clearly very clever.

Because Bruce was a bit girl crazy, his mother refused to send him to Christopher Columbus High School because it was a co-ed school. She instead sent him to an all boys school. He was always very successful in school, well-liked and even was the class president of his junior class.

Bruce went on to attend college at Lehman and subsequently earned an associate's degree in business administration with a minor in communication disorders. The thing is, with the amount of classes that he took post-degree, he could have had a doctorate. He took classes at WCC throughout his career and then post-retirement in political science and government. He enjoyed learning and furthering his knowledge.

Bruce had a 34 year law enforcement career with the Westchester County Police Department. He took such pride in his work and was a true hero to so many. He taught us that public service is noble and necessary; that one can serve with integrity and hold true to the important values. He strongly believed that it was important to give back to the community. Bruce joined the Westchester County Police in January 1983. They promoted him to sergeant in 1991 and remained a well-respected public protector throughout his 34 years of service. In May of 2016, he retired. He took such pride in his work and was a genuine hero to so many. He recognized that serving others enriched the soul.

In 1979 Bruce married Debbie. Together, they had two children: Andrew and Kristen, in September 1987. As a family, he enjoyed watching Andrew's baseball games, attending dad's races, going to car shows, taking summer vacations and hanging out in our neighborhood with neighbors. After nearly thirty years of marriage, they divorced.

Life as a bachelor for Bruce included traveling for racing, bowling, attending NASCAR races, and spending time with us and his family.

We then met, and he became the love of my life in November 2014. Together, we consolidated our families. His family became mine, mine became his, and together we were one. We spent many holidays and birthdays together, which was so much fun. We had an unbreakable bond. We enjoyed each other's company and spent so many unforgettable times together - lots of traveling, goal crushing (earning of degrees and obtaining leadership positions), and purchasing our beautiful home in ▇▇▇▇▇▇▇ this past year. Our love was undeniable and we balanced each other out so well.

I have truly been blessed to have shared my time with Bruce and the incredible family we built together. There are so many wonderful memories that we have made together each and every day as we shared our interests and passions and formed our life together.

When we met, I had never heard of autocross, but from our first conversation, it was evident that it was one of his passions. Bruce had been involved in autocross for over thirty years and loved every moment. Although the racing season went from March to November, it was a year long event. From deciding on the right car, the right tires and the right set up he was a man with a mission. I was quickly caught up in his passion and was his biggest fan. Through the years, we had been to many autocross events at many venues in many states, and I am proud to say I have become a very competent pit crew. I learned from him how to set up the car, check tire pressures, adjust shocks, how to identify a Chicago box and how to enter a tight slalom. When we walked the course and my most important job of all was to tell him how he did after each run and what he could do to go faster. With my extensive autocross knowledge I usually said, "Don't drive like a wus, no breaks and go fast". He would always laugh and smile and the next run would be faster. For those of you who have ever driven with Bruce, whether in the beloved Mini Cooper, one of the many Camaro's, a police car, or an army Humvee, it can get a little scary. Whenever I would flinch while he was driving he would say, "The United States Government trusts me. So should you". He loved teaching his Evo racing schools, whether to autocrossers or special forces at Fort Campbell.

When he wasn't racing and driving fast, he loved watching NASCAR races. Andrew and Bruce shared this passion, yet they could never agree on the best driver. They each had their favorite. Again, this was new to me and I really didn't understand the significance of driving around in circles for hundreds of miles for hours, but as we started attending NASCAR races at different venues, my appreciation grew. Andrew taught me to buy the best tickets to surprise Bruce each year. We looked forward to traveling to new venues, picking the winners and predicting the crashes. Each year, our goal was to attend a race at a new venue. We have been to Daytona a few times, Pocono, Richmond, and Charleston, and gotten sunburned and sat through many rain delays. A little unknown tidbit about Bruce is that each week he would practice the NASCAR track on his PS4 before the race on Sunday, and as we watched the race, he would compare his times and strategies with that of the NASCAR drivers.

But racing wasn't his only passion. One day, shortly after Bruce had retired, and he was taking a political science class, he decided to get involved in the politics of Peekskill. He volunteered with the republican party and his first task was to go door to door and hand out information about the candidates. That day, he met Brendan and was hooked. As with everything else, he jumped in head first. His passion for local politics and civic engagement resulted in his political group launching a talk show called Up and About with Peekskill United where he and his cronies, Luis Joe and Bob, offered political commentary on local happenings, attended momentous events, and produced segments on influential residents and business owners. Bruce became known as the "Man on the Street" and talked to everyone. His involvement then led him to become the Republican Party Chairman. I don't know if you know this, but the party chairmen are referred to as "The Honorable". Each time mail came that was addressed to the Honorable Bruce ████, he would tease me that I should be calling him "The Honorable". Through his political endeavors, I am proud to say that Bruce has been revered as a noble man who was fair and always willing to have a friendly conversation or rousing debate. Bruce was also very proud of being a member of the Westchester County Traffic and Safety Board. Whether on a highway or an autocross course where he was a Chief Safety Steward, safety was always important to him and he was honored to be chosen by the County Legislators.

Peekskill has always had a special place in his heart and, after spending thirty-four years with the WCPD serving his community, becoming part of the Peekskill Rotary was a natural fit. 'Service above self' is the motto of all members of the Rotary and one that Bruce had always embodied. He was actively involved in the Rotary and had been serving as the Secretary and looking forward to the years ahead and becoming president. Every Thursday we would talk about the Rotary Meeting and the presentations. He was so proud when Kristen presented to the Rotary on Speech

Therapy. He would always go back to that moment and always had a huge smile on his face. Bruce often spoke of all the wonderful people and programs that the Rotary funded and the contributions that the rotarians make to the community. He assisted with the Literacy Lovers, knowing that was near and dear to my heart, and bringing meals to the Jan Peak shelter was always a highlight for Bruce. On the occasions that I joined him, it was evident that he loved talking, connecting and making each person there feel respected and valued.

No matter how busy the schedule was, Wednesday nights were dedicated to bowling. For many years, Bruce was an avid bowler. He bowled in many leagues and was very competitive, and as with everything else, he did not like to lose. But bowling was also a time for family. Many of the teams he bowled on included his sister Nancy, his brother-in-law Harold and his niece's Anna and Molly. This talented group of bowlers won many championships together over the years. Bruce loved watching Anna bowl. He would travel to her tournaments and was so proud of her many achievements.She was always the best bowler in the league and he was proud to tell people she was his niece. When Harold and Nancy moved to Myrtle Beach, there was a lot of pressure when he convinced me to join the team, but with his encouragement, I did contribute to two team championships. To be honest, it was my low average that contributed because it brought down the team handicap.

Growing up in the Bronx, it was only natural that Bruce was a die hard Yankee fan. He enjoyed going to games ever since he was a little boy. One day, when we were going through his Yankee memorabilia, we found an old score card. The date on the scorecard was June 14th, 1966. That date happens to be my exact birthday, and we always joked that on the day I was born he was keeping score at the Yankee game. Bruce truly enjoyed going to a game. He loved the stadium; he loved the sausage and peppers and loved spending time with family and friends at the stadium.

So between Autocross, NASCAR, political and community events, and standing beside me at Robert and Nicky's hockey games, he was busy, but always found time to travel and we visited many places together. Bruce loved embarking on new adventures and traveling. Whether finding a cold ice rink where he would cheer on the boys or an autocross course, exploring and buying cigars for Matt in Cuba, off roading during the one rainstorm in months in Aruba, feeding iguanas in St. Maarten or relaxing on a Caribbean beach he loved to explore. As you would expect, Bruce would always strike up conversations with the locals and try to learn as much as he could about the location and culture. Bruce always valued people and made them feel special, whether they were a friend, adversary or a new acquaintance.

Bruce had a natural ability to be a leader. He inspired me in so many ways. He supported me, encouraged me, and motivated me to live my life and career to the fullest. He was always my rock.

His experiences, wisdom and leadership qualities made him the "go to man" for many people. Everyone who knew him knew that if there was any hiccup in any of our lives (a flat tire, running out of gas, work-related issues, concerns with my kids, or advice with personal relationships) Bruce was the one to call and he always solved everything, rationally and logically.

TWO

☆ ★ ☆ ★ ☆ ★ ☆ ★

The pain of losing a child never goes away. It stays with us until we meet again in the great beyond. When our children battle their demons, all we want to do is jump in and fight for them, but we can't. It's their fight. One that their own hands must win and unfortunately there's no guarantee they will. What's important is knowing we did all we could, even during our darkest hours, when we feel it wasn't enough.

☆ ★ ☆ ★ ☆ ★ ☆ ★

∞ The Story of Eight ∞

Donna's Reading

☆ ★ ☆ ★ ☆ ★ ☆ ★

Terry: So you're going to pick a pencil out of that box, rub it between both hands. I like your nails.

Donna: Thank you.

Terry: This came while you were sitting here. *points to paper* This also came while you were sitting here. *points to paper* Everything else came prior to you coming. Okay? So I don't know why, so we're going to figure it out.

Donna: Okay.

Terry: The month of February came through. Now this could be for someone living at this point, so either any day in February might mean something to you, the second of any month or the number two.

Donna: Okay.

Terry: So why would I hear February?

Donna: I don't know.

Terry: Okay. Does someone have two children?

Donna: In February?

Terry: No. It could be any day in February means something, or the second of any month, or just the number two. Sometimes if someone just gives me a number, it may mean as many children there were or I have to figure out why I heard two.

Donna: I now have two children.

Terry: You do? Okay. So there are two children left, so we'll figure it out. So this is what this girl, by the way it's a girl coming through, alright, so she's saying two. Two. So this is going to be your daughter because she's saying, "Mom, watch your stomach". Now, are you having digestive issues?

Donna: *Nods*

Terry: Oh. Okay. So this is a current event. So she has to prove it's her. She can't just show up. Okay? So if someone from the other side is going to mention something medical, it will always be okay. They never show me bad.

Donna: Right. Okay.

Terry: So I'm going to leave her here for right now. The month of April. Is she cremated?

Donna: No.

Terry: She's showing me ashes. Why is she showing me ashes? There are tissues there just in case you need them.

Donna: Her best friend passed away in April. He was cremated.

Terry: So there you go. There's your April. She's with him. That's the next month. So you know it's her. I'm very surprised that she was able to get through, to be honest with you. And then the last month is May. So either any day in May, the fifth of any month, the number five, the name Mary, Maria could be part of a name: Annmarie, Mary-Ann. So why would I hear May? Is it someone's birthday? Someone's anniversary? Does the name Mary mean anything? Could be a first or middle name.

Donna: Her grandmother on her father's side was Mary.

Terry: Okay. Is she Michelle?

Donna: Yes.

Terry: With an older woman. She's with an older woman watching over her. But she sneaks away from her because she'd rather hang here. So she's doing what she wants to do, even on the other side.

My throat, when you sat down, it felt like it became a trauma area for me. Did someone have a tube down their throat? Could someone not swallow? All of the sudden I felt my throat.

Donna: The coroner had put the tube down her throat when they did the autopsy.

Terry: Oh. Okay. Alright. So she's proving that it's her.

Donna: Well, this was as soon as I sat down.

Terry: Oh, then she knew then. Okay. She's got to be very strong willed.

Donna: Oh God yes.

Terry: She still is. She's a handful. I will say she's a handful. Extremely independent thinking. I do it my way. I'll get it done, but don't tell me how to do it.

Donna: Right.

Terry: I'll do it my way. And that is her spirit, she's saying. Now I have to ask you because she's making me feel equal to her on the other side - not with the friend - did you have any miscarriages? Because she's showing me, there's blood on the other side to her - it's her blood line so it would be you or her dad's - but I would have been equal to her in age. This is another girl that she is hanging out with. So it could have been a miscarriage or an abortion. So you may hear. You may not even know, okay?

Donna: Right.

Terry: Okay. It could have been a cousin, but it's a bloodline. She's telling me, "I'm with an equal". But she's saying equal blood. Not an equal friend because a friend would come in as the same generation.

Donna: Right.

Terry: Okay. When I was praying, my hands and feet started hurting me. Does someone suffer from numbing of the hands and feet, pain in the hands and feet?

Donna: Me.

Terry: Oh. It's you. So she's very connected to her mom. So she's just connecting me with your energy. Okay. Who's the drinker?

Donna: My ex-husband.

Terry: Okay. He's still living, right?

Donna: No.

Terry: Oh. He passed.

Donna: He passed.

Terry: Okay. Is that her dad?

Donna: Yes.

Terry: Okay. I don't know why. And the reason I asked if he was still living - see where the drinker is up here? *points to the paper*

Donna: Yes.

Terry: So she didn't go there yet (to see her dad). She'll visit, but not yet. Okay. She'll visit. But this older woman, whoever she is… Now your mom is still with us?

Donna: My mom is still with me. Her biological grandmother, my ex-husband's mother, is gone, but she also was very close to my new husband's mother, who's gone.

Terry: That's who she's with. That's why I asked is Mom here because she's telling me it goes through the mother's energy, which would be you.

Donna: She was very close.

Terry: That's who's watching her. Because it didn't make sense to me because she's saying sometimes she skips this woman to come here, but if this woman is the drinker's mom, then she would have brought her to the drinker already. But she hasn't yet. So I pick up the energy, not the blood. Did this older woman - so they're touching my heart. Did someone have heart issues?

Donna: She did.

Terry: Okay. So she has to prove it. She can't just show up.

Donna: Yes. She did.

Terry: Okay. Is this less than a year?

Donna: Is this less than a year?

Terry: Yeah.

Donna: Tomorrow's a month.

Terry: Oh no. Oh my God. So sorry.

Donna: That's why I was so upset last week.

Terry: Oh my God. So sorry. Oh, my God. But I have to tell you she's already a handful. Did she wear glasses?

Donna: Yes.

Terry: Did they not fit her right?

Donna: They weren't hers.

Terry: Oh that's why. Because she's complaining about the glasses.They don't fit me right. The tattoo - what is she talking about?

Donna: Her's?

Terry: I don't know. She says, "Now you can mention the tattoo". I don't want to piss her off.

Donna: She wanted to get matching tattoos. When she was here. She wanted it here and fought her to do it here because I said I'm an older woman that works in an office. It doesn't look right. Let's decide somewhere else. And then after she went I decided I'm doing the tattoo.

Terry: Alright. So she knows that. See? You can't make this shit up, Donna.

Donna: I know.

Terry: It has to be her. Okay? Who bruises very easily?

Donna: Me.

Terry: Okay. Wow. She's really attached to her mom. You don't have any bruises on you, so I wouldn't know that, but she does this to me. She says, "Now you'll bruise". So she knows my signs. Do you have a house phone?

Donna: Yes.

Terry: Okay. So listen to what's going to happen. That phone may ring. You may pick it up and hear static or absolutely nothing. That's her. She's still around you. She's saying, "I'm still around. Still around you".

Aha Moment: A few years after the reading Donna told me this happened to her one night while she was making dinner.

Terry: Did she know Rob, Bob, Bobbie, Robert?

Donna: Yes.

Terry: So how did she know this name?

Donna: Living?

Terry: I don't know. So this name came in before you even got here. Right near her, so I have to figure out why.

Donna: Rob is my husband's brother.

Terry: Okay. Is he living?

Donna: Yes.

Terry: Okay. So she wants to go to him. Again, if they're going to show me something, it will be okay. So if someone is suffering from something, you kind of want them to mention it. But she goes from here to here to tell you - are you Italian?

Donna: Yes.

Terry: Okay because she said like agita, not heart. She used agita, not heartburn. So it's something from here up.

Donna: Yes.

Terry: So when you hear about it, your daughter is saying, "It's not a coincidence because I already told you about that Mom."

Donna: Right.

Terry: Diabetic nerve... Diabetic. Sorry. Okay. Who's diabetic?

Donna: My mother.

Terry: Okay, so she wants to talk about diabetic nerve damage. So I don't know if Mom's feet...

Donna: Yes.

Terry: Oh. So she knows about that. So she watches over her grandmother carefully because her grandmother is suffering two deaths right now.

Donna: Oh my God.

Terry: So why would she tell me that?

Donna: My father died in September.

Terry: I didn't write it down; the September.

Donna: And Michelle.

Terry: Okay. There you go. So that's how she wanted to tell me she's with her grandfather. "Because my grandmother is suffering two deaths." I mean, you are too, but she wanted to go to the grandmother because first she went to the diabetes to prove it's her.

Donna: Yes.

Terry: My nose hurts. Did someone break their nose or have an injury at one time? Remember, it doesn't have to be the way I passed, but I would have had to suffer with it. Because I feel pain just in my face and I don't know why.

Donna: She used to snort drugs.

Terry: Okay. That's why.

Donna: And I found out recently that one of the things she had tried to do to get high was to snort Xanax.

Terry: Okay. There you go. Then that's why my nose would feel different. Because it goes from my nose to here *points to face*. Okay. So she's just owning it. That's what she's doing. They walked over - so when I say "they" it's everyone that showed up so far - to my refrigerator. Now that will not be a coincidence because they know what my signs are. Did someone have to replace a refrigerator, were talking about a refrigerator or a kitchen appliance?

Donna: No. You told me that the last time?

Terry: I read you before?

Donna: Yes.

Terry: When did I read you?

Donna: For my father.

Terry: Oh good. I don't remember. Okay. So what's with that refrigerator? They keep going to the refrigerator.

Donna: My sister-in-law had an issue with her refrigerator and my husband fixed it.

Terry: There you go. Okay. So it's a current event.

Donna: Yup.

Terry: I'm sorry I didn't recognize you.

Donna: That's okay.

Terry: But it's better for me if I don't.

Donna: Yes. No. It's better.

Terry: You know it's clean and it's not repetitive.

Donna: Exactly. Yes. Absolutely.

Terry: Because it's very important that you know that. Don't let it turn into a family feud. That's what your daughter just said to me. Is someone arguing with someone or is there a chance of a family feud?

Donna: Yes.

Terry: "So Mom", she's saying, "don't let this turn into a family feud because you don't need it."

Donna: Right.

Terry: Did you find her writings yet? Did you know she used to write? So it could be writing feelings or…

Donna: I know she used to write feelings, and I found a sticky note that said, "I'm sorry Mommy. Love me".

Terry: Okay. There you go. That's her writing. So you found it. Okay. Alright. So she has to keep proving it's her. The flag. She's showing me an American flag. So when I see an American flag, either someone actually has this flag at the house or someone was or is in the military. So why is she showing me the flag?

Donna: My father was in the military.

Terry: Okay. So he keeps a very close eye on her. He also wants you to know she's listening to a lot of music on the other side. It's therapeutic because she tends to not have a ton of patience and gets frustrated easily. So the music is magical for her on the other side and she's taking care of outside animals right now. So was she an animal person?

Donna: Yes.

Terry: But it's more for her the outside animals. Like the bunnies and the birds.

Donna: Oh God. Yes.

Terry: Okay. Because the others have homes and everybody likes them, but - this is according to your daughter - people tend to forget the outside animals so she says, "Mom. You know how I used to say that the animals talk to me". Or she would feel how they felt.

Donna: Yes.

Terry: There they actually do.

Donna: Okay.

Terry: You know she had demons most of her life, she's saying.

Donna: Yes.

Terry: "And no one could have helped me, but you saved me a couple of times", she's saying. "But this was meant to be this way."

Donna: Oh. *Cries*

Terry: I know. It's easy for them to say. Look, my sister lost her son March first.

Donna: I'm sorry.

Terry: He turned thirty-four February twenty-eighth. He passed on the first. Six hours. So I know that it's easy for them to say, but I have to repeat what I hear. Who's in the medical field? Who's in the medical field? Was someone working in a hospital or is someone studying to be a nurse? Did someone talk about it? Do I work in a dentist's office? Is someone an EMT? Or was an EMT?

Donna: I do medical billing.

Terry: Okay. So you're in the medical field as far as she's concerned. Okay. So it's so funny. She's only bringing me to you. She mentioned two siblings, but she talks about you and your mom because I guess this is what you need. I don't know. This is what you need. She mentions the name Steve. So when I hear that name: Steve, Steven, Steph, Stephanie or last name Stevenson. So why would she mention this?

Donna: The only Stephanie I know is my son's girlfriend.

Terry: Was she just around you?

Donna: We were just together.

Terry: Okay. Current event. That's why. It's funny. I'm saying to her, "Do you want to say hello to your siblings?" The next thing I hear is Steve, because she knows where I go with Steve if I just hear a name. Especially if they're not on the other side, then I don't know male or female. She said, "No. Just Steve".

Donna: Right.

Terry: And she was there when Stephanie…

Donna: When we were together.

Terry: "Mom, I only have to go to the cemetery when people visit me. I hate going to the cemetery, Mom. Can't you do something else?"

Donna: *Laughs*

Terry: And that is the truth. They only go to the cemetery…

Donna: Okay.

Terry: My head is killing me right now. So… Okay. She stopped my timer. She did a twenty-seven. *Timer stopped at twenty-seven minutes* Okay. Thank you. Never a coincidence when it stops on a number. Does the number twenty-seven mean something to you? Am I near the twenty-seventh of any month? Or does, specifically, February seventh or July second mean something? See, it's working again, but when they stop it on a certain number, it's never a coincidence. Did someone pass near the twenty-seventh of a month?

Donna: She passed on the twenty-third.

Terry: Okay. No. Not her, she's saying. Was she June twenty-third?

Donna: She passed on June twenty-third.

Terry: It's so funny. She said that's my sister Donna's birthday.

Donna: Oh.

Terry: She's saying to me, "I passed on your sister's birthday". And my sister, Donna, is the one who lost her son. But she's talking about someone near the age of twenty-seven.

Donna: My son is twenty-seven.

Terry: There you go. Okay. It's never a coincidence when they stop my clock. My timer is working beautifully now. So she wants to reach out to that person.

Donna: To Joey.

Terry: So that's it. She's showing me plantings. Did someone recently do plantings or…

Donna: We're going to do a garden.

Terry: Where?

Donna: In our yard.

Terry: Thank God.

Donna: We've had people that brought us beautiful plants for outside and we're going to make it Michelle's garden.

Terry: Okay. Good. With a stone. She's talking about a stone. What stone is she talking about?

Donna: We're going to make a pavement patio out of stones.

Terry: There you go. Now, she's saying, "Mom, do yourself a favor. You need to get something that stays green all year because I know you. If it snows and everything dies, you're going to say, 'just like my daughter'. I'm greenery. I go on forever." So you need to get an evergreen. Even if it's just a small little tree.

Donna: Right.

Terry: So at least you know things around my daughter are going to sleep, because they'll come back, but my daughter is the green. It's the green.

Donna: Okay.

Terry: "Mom, you have to do the holidays." Were you talking about not doing them?

Donna: *Nods*

Terry: Okay. Okay. She can't interfere with your decision.

Donna: Right.

Terry: She's just giving you her opinion. That's all she's doing. You do what you have to do for yourself. Okay? Are you my coffee drinker?

Donna: Yes.

Terry: Do you have it alone in the morning?

Donna: Mm hmm.

Terry: I think that's when she's with you the longest. Did you know that?

Donna: I play her music box every morning and a few times I saw what I thought was an orb.

Terry: There you go. That's her. She just confirmed that. Okay? So you knew that. Well, you felt it. Perfect. You see that feeling you had? "Oh, it was an orb. I feel it." That's *them* speaking to you. And it was. And then it's not even a coincidence that your dad mentions music with her. You listen to a music box so you see how all this ties together?

Donna: It connects.

Terry: Yeah. She's happy he's there, but he's up her ass already.

Donna: *Laughs*

Terry: She's already complaining. "I can't go anywhere." So was that the type of relationship?

Donna: Yes.

Terry: Or her personality?

Donna: Yes.

Terry: Okay. The kid, and I think I'm male… My head is hurting for different reasons. I thought I was going somewhere else. I'm asking her because it's hurting me a little too much. Did someone die in an accident where my head was my trauma area? Did I hit my head? Was I shot in my head? It's my head. And it's quick. Boom and it hurts.

Donna: Not that I know of.

Terry: Okay. That's your "Aha" moment. Because when you find out who it is, like I could have been on a motorcycle and fell off the motorcycle and this is how I passed, this one is the way that I passed. This one is male. Equal to her, so in her generation. Generation is ten years. When you remember who it is, "I'm with this person also".

Donna: So that person is already passed.

Terry: Yes. This one's passed.

Donna: Okay.

Terry: And this is one of the rare times that a spirit will tell me this was the way this person passed.

Donna: Okay.

Aha Moment: Donna got in touch with me to let me know she figured out who this person was. The son of a close family friend passed years before the reading due to a gunshot to the head.

Terry: Other than her, she's giving me the sign of drugs, which is my right nostril. Why is she doing this to me?

Donna: She overdosed.

Terry: Oh. That's how she passed. So then I understand what she's doing. Your daughter is owning it.

Donna: She always did.

Terry: Yeah. This is what I did. She's talking about Tuesdays. Is someone off on Tuesdays? Was Tuesday a certain special day?

Donna: No.

Terry: The restaurant Tuesdays? There's something with Tuesdays. Please keep that in mind. Do you know what day she passed on?

Donna: She passed on a Sunday.

Terry: Oh. The Lord's day. And she was born on what day?

Donna: She was born on June sixteenth, ninety-four.

Terry: Our Lady of Mount Carmel by the way. Oh, so she's giving me religious days. Isn't that funny? Although that's not her.

Donna: No.

Terry: At all, but it is now. So our Lady of Mount Carmel was July sixteenth.

Donna: June sixteenth.

Terry: Oh. June sixteenth. No. Was it a Tuesday?

Donna: Her birthday? I don't know.

Terry: Okay. She's talking about Tuesday. So I hear Walter, but Walter could be Wally, Willie, a "W", even Billy because Billy is short for Willy or William. Why would she mention this name?

Donna: We have family members who are William.

Terry: Okay. So she's mentioning them just as a confirmation. And Val. Who's Val, Valerie? Actually Val is with her. And this Val, so if they're not going to give me their name, they're going to give me the name of someone living how they know you through. So your daughter is saying, "Tell my mom I'm bringing in her", meaning your "equal". So this is a female on the other side that could be a sister, sister-in-law, cousin, friend.

Donna: Val?

Terry: So let's work backwards. Okay? Val could be living and this woman is giving you the name of how she knows you. How do you know a Val / Valerie?

Donna: I have my mother's older family friend Valerie.

Terry: Now, Valerie, did she lose a daughter? Because this one would be equal to you in your generation.

Donna: No.

Terry: Alright. So just keep it in mind. There's this woman.

Aha Moment: Years after this reading Donna let me know she figured out who Val was. Her cousin, who was about eight years younger than her, passed before Michelle.

Terry: Your daughter is very friendly on the other side. She loves her people. She prefers her animals because they used to take away her pain. That's what she's telling me. "It's not so much when I was in body form that I took away their pain, although I understood them. They took my pain away." So this was going on for years, Donna.

Donna: Yes. I know.

Terry: Okay. She had demons with her at all times.

Donna: Yes.

Terry: And Archangel Michael, specifically, went to go see her. It's never a coincidence when they mention a certain archangel. So with Michael, I know her name is Michelle, but usually I go to Michael or Michelle because that's Archangel Michael, the month of September, but I already know that's your father so it would have to be something different, or an affiliation with a police officer or firefighter.

Donna: My son's birthday is in September. My other son.

Terry: Okay. It's never a coincidence when they bring in a certain archangel over another.

Donna: Right.

Terry: "Even though I always had it in the back of my mind that I could stop," so her mind was so heavy for her, "this was an accident."

Donna: Thank God. Okay. That was one of the things I wanted to know. If she did it on purpose.

Terry: No. That's what she's saying. "Even though I always had it in the back of my mind because I couldn't take it sometimes, this was an accident. I didn't mean to do it. Because I wouldn't do it to you, Mom."

Donna: Right.

Terry: That's what she's saying. "I wouldn't do it to you. And the timing sucked. I wouldn't do it." So you have to know that. That's very important to her, that it was an accident. I hope they put that on her death certificate. What's the matter?

Donna: Wait. Didn't you say something about July?

Terry: Yeah. That's Our Lady of Mount Carmel.

Donna: Right, but then you said something about dates. My son's getting married on July third of next year and she was supposed to be in the wedding.

Terry: Okay. There you go. So she wouldn't have done that. She's just proved she wouldn't have done it. And that's Our Lady of Mount Carmel's month. So Carmines, Carmin, Carmella, Milly's. Yeah, because she mentioned July to me. You said June, but I heard July.

Donna: I forgot about it.

Terry: Okay. So these are "Aha" moments, Donna. But on the death certificate, they did not put suicide.

Donna: No. It's still pending.

Terry: Okay. She's saying, "I didn't do it on purpose". Other than coke, did she also do pills?

Donna: Yes.

Terry: Did she take the pills?

Donna: She took pills, but she was a heroin addict.

Terry: Yeah. Okay. So you know, at one point, she was trying to stop.

Donna: Yes. She had been clean for three years.

Terry: Okay. That's the problem because when you go back to it you think your body is used to what it was used to three years ago and it's not. People don't realize that and then it just overtakes you. Her heart will be included in that death certificate, that's what she's saying. She felt the heart; a heart attack also. She's saying, "Mom, I did not do this on purpose, but you can be mad at me because I understand when you get mad it's healing. So you can be mad at me".

Donna: I am.

Terry: Alright. Good. "Just don't hate me", she's saying.

Donna: I don't.

Terry: "Just don't hate me." You know what's funny with the February other than the two remaining children, did you know you're wearing the February stone? This. This is an amethyst.

Donna: This was hers.

Terry: There you go. It's the February birthstone, the amethyst. Oh, that's why she mentions it as well.

Donna: This was hers.

Terry: That's very powerful, February. This makes even more sense. You know I'm known as the spiritual medium because there are some things I know, spiritually, because I had an aunt who passed - it's actually in my book. When I was three, she was one of the first spirits that came to me. She actually took me to heaven with her. One thing I learned is Archangel Michael - she keeps going to Archangel Michael by the way - while he wears blue, the aura from the sword is purple. And that's when he is actively protecting someone. The aura from the stone is purple, so that is the purple stone, so he was even protecting her when she was in body form. Because certain colors have certain vibrational energy attached to them. Did she live with you?

Donna: Yeah.

Terry: "Right now you find that comforting," she's saying. "You may not in years to come."

Donna: Right.

Terry: And it's okay to sell.

Donna: Okay.

Terry: That's what she wants you to know. "Mom, when you get the feeling to sell, I'm not attached to the house. I'm attached to you. So you could do a garden wherever you want." And she's saying, "I love being in the garden". She would rather you go there than to the cemetery. She would rather you go to the garden to speak to her, but you could always do another garden. The garden is going to be for you, not for her, although she is going to be there a lot. She wants solar lights near it so that it's never dark. She doesn't like the dark. So you could have solar lights. Also, do you have one at her tombstone?

Donna: A good friend of ours just put one there.

Terry: She wants to thank you for that. That's a pretty current event. So you see how she still "is", she's saying. Do you have a birthday coming up or an anniversary coming up?

Donna: September is our anniversary; our wedding anniversary.

Terry: Because you forgot to say that when it came to Archangel Michael, she's saying. She's telling me to go back to September. You forgot about that.

Donna: Yup.

Terry: Okay. Who's the left-handed person?

Donna: My husband.

Terry: She wants to acknowledge him big time. Are you having problems with him right now?

Donna: Kind of.

Terry: Yeah, she's saying. She knows. She doesn't want you to confirm any further. She tells me this is a family matter. "I just want you to tell my mom I know."

Donna: Right.

Terry: Did she ever wear anything with lace?

Donna: Only when she was a baby.

Terry: Did someone have something? She's showing me lace and I don't know why she's showing me lace.

Donna: Yes. The gown she wore for my wedding. The top was black lace, and that's what we buried her in.

Terry: There you go. That's probably why she wanted to reach out to your husband as well. She's just not ready yet for this. No one takes shit on the other side. But I really don't want to because how long ago did he pass though?

Donna: Probably about seven years ago.

Terry: Okay. So he's on another level already. She's on the first level. There are seven levels. He's probably on the second level. She can't go to the second level until… so prayers move them along. Once she's on the second level, she will go visit him. He can come down to the first, but he hasn't. And I will tell you he hasn't.

Donna: Okay.

Terry: I don't think she's ready yet for that.

Donna: Right.

Terry: "I want to be as close to my mom as possible." Then even if she goes to the second level, she can still come and go as she wants.

Donna: Okay.

Terry: But right now, the only person she's really consumed with is her mom. Did she also suffer from anxiety?

Donna: Yes.

Terry: Because she gives me the pain right through the center of my heart. That's the anxiety sign for me. Did she ever do any form of self harm?

Donna: She used to cut.

Terry: Okay. Because that's what I'm doing. I didn't want to say it.

Donna: She used to cut.

Terry: Okay. Because the pain would make my mind stop. She really was going to kill herself at one point. She's saying, "I was going to do this years ago, but I didn't because I couldn't do it to my mom. But I swear," she's telling me, "I didn't do it this time. This was an accident". That's torturous. *Points to paper* This is a cute little eight. What's in August, the eighth of any month, or the number eight? Now, could it be a family that has six children to make it a family of eight?

Donna: My husband's family. There were six children.

Terry: Okay. So she wants to go to him for a purer reason now. "You know, Mom, the energy in his back is off," she's telling you. Did you know that?

Donna: Yes.

Terry: Oh. You know it. Okay. And you know he's cranky, and he's hurting.

Donna: I know.

Terry: "Because he loved my mom and I loved him." But I don't think she gave him a full chance. Maybe in the beginning. Maybe it took her a while or something. I don't know, but she says, "And I loved him". Because I don't deliver messages of love unless they insist and they usually insist if someone doubted it or maybe there was a problem in the relationship. So she wants you to know. Okay, so the eight is small, but he's not small for her. This is a major player in her life and he'll always be a major player.

Donna: Yes. He was.

Terry: He cries. You don't know that. You don't know it.

Donna: Okay.

Terry: I think he's crying in the shower or in the car. Because I need to be strong for you. But he cries. Don't think his heart is cold or he's callous. That's why she's mentioning it to you.

Donna: Okay.

Terry: But you don't have to tell him. She's saying, "You don't tell him you know. Alright Mom?"

Donna: Yeah.

Terry: Who had the breast issues? I'm living. Now this is going to be good. Well, it's going to have a good outcome. And you may not know it yet. I'm not going to you. Someone may have found a lump or some breast issues. It's only an issue. It'll be okay.

Donna: Right. Okay.

Terry: Have you started taking pictures of the clouds yet?

Donna: No.

Terry: She's coming through in the clouds. You actually may just be driving and look at a cloud and if you get the gut feeling, you might have your phone and take a picture. Then you wait three days and then you'll see. But that is her. Also that music box, she's going to let it go off on her own. She's saying, "I might only be strong enough right now to do one or two notes". You may be having coffee and not put it on yourself and you'll hear a note or two. "That's going to be me, Mom."

Aha Moment: Donna let me know about a month after her reading she was making coffee and thinking about playing the music box after the coffee was made when it went off by itself.

Terry: Also, one of the windows needs replacement or is giving you a hard time.

Donna: Oh my God.

Terry: What's with the window?

Donna: We were replacing a window in her bedroom.

Terry: Alright. Did you do it?

Donna: It's happening Tuesday.

Terry: When?

Donna: Tuesday. *Gasps* Oh my God!

Terry: And there you go. Your daughter thinks she's hot shit on the other side.

Donna: *Laughs*

Terry: Because she just went, "Ta-da!"

Donna: *Laughs* Oh God. I love her so much.

Terry: And that's the problem. I can't even imagine.

Donna: I know.

Terry: You know. Because your life will be measured in before Michelle passed and after.

Donna: I know.

Terry: You will never heal. You're not supposed to heal. Especially with a mother. You're not going to heal. We all scar into a person you need to be to exist and, on the other hand, you do have children and grandchildren coming. Who's the Jewish lady she's talking about?

Donna: My son's future wife is partially Jewish.

Terry: *Talking to Michelle* Okay. I will ask her. So I have to ask you about the book and the gift. Please remind me of this.

Donna: Okay.

Terry: Who's Jill, Jilly, Julia? I hear "J.L." I'm living; not passed.

Donna: I don't know.

Terry: Jules, Julie, Julia, Jillian. Was I working with her? So I'm equal to your daughter. Okay. Who's Tom? Tom. Tommy.

Donna: My uncle.

Terry: Okay. And is he on the other side?

Donna: No. He's here.

Terry: Okay. She mentions Tom. She went visiting. So now she visits. She's not afraid to visit. She goes there just to see. "I want to check up on things," she's saying. So was she the type of person who didn't enjoy going to people's houses and you missed out on stuff?

Donna: Yes.

Terry: And you didn't have a lot of people at the house because of her?

Donna: Well we did, but when it was time for us to go to people's houses and she was included, she wouldn't want to go.

Terry: Okay. But she's doing it now. Good. Just so you know. Who used to have to eat through a straw or I couldn't chew food?

Donna: Her grandfather on her father's side.

Terry: He's on the other side, though, this one.

Donna: Yes.

Terry: Alright. He comes in to say hello to you. "I want to say hello to you. We're all with her. Know that your daughter is never alone. The only time she's alone is when she's in the house during your morning coffee because she's home, so she's not really alone. She's with you. And that's where we trust her." You know she won't feel lonely or scared.

Even when she goes to Tommy's house, one of them goes with her. She mentions the name Vin.

Donna: Vin?

Terry: Vin. Vinny. Vincent. Was there a Vin, Vinny, Vincent that's around one of the surviving kids? So here's the message. "Mom, I don't really care for his energy." So I know he's living. Do you have boys?

Donna: Boys. Older boys.

Terry: Not the daughter. Okay. That's what she's saying. So I feel, boys. One of the boys. One of the brothers. Either they're not dealing the right way or are bothering one of the brothers. She doesn't like the energy. She's saying, "Mom, it's not that they're bringing in drugs or doing what I did". She says, "You know, in rehab, Mom, we learn where our new dealers are". Just so you know.

Donna: You said to remind you.

Terry: Yes. Let me go through this first. So you know I promise God that anyone I read I would ask them when they find themselves totally alone to offer up three very informal prayers, all for people living. So it's for someone you care about, someone you don't even know, or someone you know who's a lost soul and someone you don't care for or you don't trust. And the prayer for that one goes something like, "Dear God, please let them find their way, but keep them away from me". So you're going to wish them well first and then create the boundary. Why does she want you to go for a haircut? Were you thinking of going for a haircut?

Donna: Well, I need to go for a dye job.

Terry: No. Not a dye job. She's saying get it cut. Were you complaining that this hair is too long or needs shaping?

Donna: It needs shaping. Yeah.

Terry: Okay. She's saying, "You'll feel a little better Mom". Now, the book. This book is my second book. In my second book, I choose eight families and what I do is I have the surviving family members write about the loss of their loved ones as they were. In your case as a baby, as a kid growing up, you know, where you bring them right to the point of before they passed over and then I include the reading. So she's telling me to ask you, do you want her memorialized in the book?

Donna: Oh. Yes.

Terry: Okay. So I'll send you information and all that stuff. We can change her name if you want. It's fine.

Donna: Nope. I'm comfortable with that.

Terry: Okay. And then we'll include parts of the reading. Not the full reading. The major parts, like I love what she did with that Tuesday. Like how they connect things to prove. This stone is very powerful. That's why I asked you if there was something coming up for you. Your daughter is giving you this. It's yours. You can put it near her music box if you want. You can put it in her garden if you want.

Donna: Yes.

Terry: That's from your daughter. Because she called me ma'am, which I know I'm old, but she didn't have to call me ma'am. She said, "Do you think you could give that to my mom?" I always say yes to those who have passed over.

Donna: Thank you.

Terry: Don't thank me.

Donna: Thank you Michelle.

Terry: Thank her because she wants to give you a present. That is an extremely powerful stone.

Donna: What is it?

Terry: It's the amethyst. It has a lot of prayers on it. She wanted to make sure you always had a gift

from her, even past her passing. So you have
something tangible from her.

Donna: Thank you Michelle.

A Letter From Donna

☆ ★ ☆ ★ ☆ ★ ☆ ★

Hi Terry,

When I had my reading with you in July, you asked me to write about Michelle so you could put it into your new book. I'm sorry it took me so long. The story kept going in the wrong direction. I'm not sure if this is what you are looking for. I hope it's not too late. My reading was under the name Donna ███████ on 7/22/19.

Thank you,

Donna

Michelle DeRuvo was a beautiful girl, both inside and out. She cared more for others than she did for herself. She was a loving girl who always tried to make people smile and laugh, especially during their times of trouble. Michelle had some demons, even as a young girl. She used to cut herself on the top of her legs and arms. As she got older, she got involved with drugs, which was ultimately what ended her life at twenty-five years old.

Michelle loved animals and always wanted to take care of them. She used to say she connected with animals. When she was a little girl, she and her friend found an abandoned baby squirrel. She helped nurse it back to health and used to carry him in the hood of her sweatshirt. She used to say she loved connecting with animals more than people because animals made her feel peace.

Michelle had a very good friend, TJ, who passed in April prior to Michelle. He was cremated. During my reading, it was confirmed she was with her friend who always wanted to be by her side and that Michelle looked to break away, even on the other side.

Michelle was very attached to my parents as well. We lived with them when my children were small. During my reading, Michelle stated she goes to check in on Grandma because she suffered two losses. My Mom lost my dad in September and then we lost Michelle in July. Michelle was very close to her Grandma Sandy during both their lives. They nicknamed themselves the smoking buddies.

After Michelle's passing, we decided to plant a memorial garden in her honor and named it "Michelle's Garden". During my reading, Michelle mentioned she wanted us to place lights in the garden, which, of course, we did. Michelle never liked the dark, even when she was older.

During my reading, Michelle kept referring to the day Tuesday and I could not understand why. She brought up a window. Michelle knew of an installation before she passed. As we discussed the window at my reading, I remembered the window, which was in Michelle's bathroom, was being installed the following Tuesday.

Michelle was full of love and energy and had a giving heart. I am grateful to her for asking Terry to discuss having Michelle memorialized in her book. Before the end of my reading, Michelle asked Terry to give me a gift from her. She asked that Terry give me the amethyst egg that was on her table. I keep it next to Michelle's music box on the counter in my kitchen. One day while listening, which I did every morning for the first year she was gone, I was speaking to Michelle. I told her I needed to know she was okay and still with me. As I passed the music box and gifted egg, there was a ball of light. It was the size of a lemon and white in color. It was bouncing up and down and side to side next to the music box. The song playing was "You Are My Sunshine" which I sang to Michelle since birth. The ball of light continued to dance to the music until it stopped playing. This was Michelle's sign to me. I will always treasure it and the beautiful gift given to me during my reading.

☆ ★ ☆ ★ ☆ ★ ☆ ★

If you or someone you know is struggling with addiction, help is a phone call or text away. You're stronger than you think you are. You can do this. You're not alone.

The National Drug Helpline is open to any individual dealing with addiction issues, including family members and other loved ones. Resources are available for those struggling with any addictive substance, including alcohol, and professionals are available to help 24/7/365 at 1-844-289-0879.

Parents and other caregivers can reach out to the Partnership for Drug-Free Kids at 1-855-378-4373, to be connected with information and assistance dealing with children's addiction issues. Live services are available during regular hours only, but concerned guardians can reach the hotline by email and by text.

☆ ★ ☆ ★ ☆ ★ ☆ ★

THREE

☆ ★ ☆ ★ ☆ ★ ☆ ★

When we pass and cross over to the other side, we leave our heavy energy behind and become one with the light. Unfortunately, those we left behind don't have it that easy. They can carry the weight of their anger until their own dying days unless they find a way to release it, whether it be by prayer, screaming into the abyss or simply writing a letter to those they feel wronged them. Healing can be the difference between finding heaven on Earth or continuing to live in a perpetual hell here on Earth.

☆ ★ ☆ ★ ☆ ★ ☆ ★

∞ The Story of Eight ∞

Sheri's Reading

☆ ★ ☆ ★ ☆ ★ ☆ ★

Terry: Pencils are in that box. Choose one. Rub it between both hands. The month of December. So at this point, it could be for someone living. What does any day in December, the twelfth of any month, the number twelve, the names Lou, Louis, Lucille, Lucia, Luis - because for me this is Saint Lucy's month? So why would I hear December? Is it someone's birthday?

Sheri: Well, it was my dad's birthday.

Terry: That's how he comes in. It's so funny. I knew dad passed, so my prayer was, "I know she's coming for you. Don't just let me mention you. You have to go along and play with me". Where's the picture of him in his sunglasses?

Sheri: I have so many pictures of him.

Terry: It almost looks like I'm doing a pose. To me it looks like dark glasses, so I'm going to go with sunglasses.

Sheri: I have a picture of him because he drove the ambulance. I have a picture of him by the ambulance and he has the sunglasses on. He was outside.

Terry: There you go. Where is that picture?

Sheri: It's downstairs in my house.

Terry: Loves that picture.

Sheri: Does he? I had it blown up after he passed away.

Terry: He goes down there a lot. So Dad so far is listening to me and giving me things that I wouldn't know because I did have the pleasure of meeting him in body form. He reminds me of that. I like what he's doing. The month of January. What does any day in January…

Sheri. There's so much. There's so much in January.

Terry: Oh. So it's a family month?

Sheri: Well, he passed in January.

Terry: He did? So you know what? Let's stick with that.

Sheri: Also with December; my mother died in December.

Terry: Okay. He's with her. He said no disrespect to anyone, but of course I'm going to go to the other side - I'm not staying alone. Who is Carol?

Sheri: That's my sister-in-law. That's my brother's wife.

Terry: Okay. So he goes to that family as well.

Sheri: I'm sure. Yeah.

Terry: So that's okay. The last month, although he wanted me to do four months, but the last month is November. What does any day in November, the eleventh of any month, or the number eleven mean to you?

Sheri: It's my daughter's birthday.

Terry: Okay. Why does he say he goes to Florida? Is there family in Florida?

Sheri: His brother is in Florida.

Terry: So he goes there as well. He wants you to know.

Sheri: And my daughter just moved back from Florida.

Terry: Oh, she was living in Florida?

Sheri: One of my daughters moved back from Florida.

Terry: Oh good. He's happy about that.

Sheri: Yup. So are we.

Terry: He puts the medical field out here. Is someone working in a hospital?

Sheri: My daughter, the one that moved back from Florida, is a medical assistant.

Terry: Okay. There you go. So he's just confirming who he's talking about. Again, I know it's him on the other side, so give me things I don't know. Did he have sores or veins on his feet? Sorry. His legs. I'm not even looking at his feet. Was there a problem with the leg or sores? Was it like bulging?

Sheri: Well, when he had the cancer...

Terry: Oh. He had cancer. That I didn't know.

Sheri: Yeah. He had cancer. When he had cancer, he spent his last few months at Rosary Hill, down in Hawthorne. That's how we noticed. We knew how bad he was. We would look at his legs - the swelling.

Terry: There you go. The swelling. Alright so the energy in his legs was off.

Sheri: The water. The edema. You knew.

Terry: You could see it.

Sheri: You knew it.

Terry: Alright. There you go. But he's also telling me he had heart issues.

Sheri: He did. He did, but he would tell you he really thought the heart was going to kill him and it didn't.

Terry: No. That's what he's saying, "Because my heart..." and he said "issues". He didn't say "the problem". He just said issues.

Sheri: He had issues. He had stents. He kept on top with the cardiologist. He did everything you were supposed to do, in general. Even with winding up with liver cancer. He had a thing called hemochromatosis - too much iron in the blood. He found out when my son was born and my son is going to be twenty-one. He went and had his blood drawn and had everything done. They never gave him sonograms of his liver to check to see if he had tumors because it affects the liver. So we were really surprised by this. He really thought the heart was going to kill him.

Terry: Yeah. No. It didn't. Who's Jack, Jackson, Jackie?

Sheri: Jack was his dog.

Terry: On the other side?

Sheri: Yes. Now. Yes. He only lasted maybe eight months after my father died.

Terry: He's with Jack.

Sheri: *Laughs* Of course.

Terry: Jack is having a great time.

Sheri: Yup. Jack we feel died of a broken heart.

Terry: He did. And he felt bad for the dog because, according to dad, who else did this dog have? I know he was married, but he doesn't put the dog's energy near his earth wife.

Sheri: Really, the sad part is my sister - because my father remarried after my mother and he had two kids. They're my sister and brother. It was her dog, but it was Dad's. She moved away, so it was Dad's dog.

Terry: Oh, did she?

Sheri: It was Dad's dog. I have pictures of when he got sick when he was still at home. That dog was just on top of him. That dog died of a broken heart.

Terry: "I don't want to say I'm so happy I'm on the other side. But I am happy. And don't worry about it. I will dance with you again." Now, did he ever dance with you?

Sheri: Just at my wedding. But it's funny because the last time I saw you you asked why does he ask about dancing?

Terry: Oh. Did I? Did I read you after he passed?

Sheri: Yes.

Terry: See, I won't even remember that.

Sheri: It was only a couple of months after he passed.

Terry: No!

Sheri: He died in January. You read me at my house in March. He would say to me, because of how the tumors were affecting him, because they were all over the place. We took him to the hospital and when they would give him the medicine, he hid a lot from us like the pain and all that and he would say to me, "Ah, don't worry, Sheri. I could do the jig. I could dance."

Terry: Oh, so dance. That's why he's saying that. So that is his confirmation.

Sheri: And I knew he was lying. You know what I mean? I knew he was in pain. I knew he was lying, but he said, "Don't worry, Sheri".

Terry: What's the picture that keeps getting crooked or falling off the wall? Or were you just trying to hang something?

Sheri: I haven't hung anything, but I fix pictures all the time. I have OCD.

Terry: Oh. You do? I didn't know that. So you are near the pictures on the wall. So he sees this. He thinks you're crazy, by the way.

Sheri: I know.

Terry: He makes my head hurt. But I don't think it has to do with him. So when my head hurts, it's a trauma area. Remember, it doesn't have to be the way I passed, but I would have had to suffer with it. Who had the head injury, the stroke, the aneurysm, alzheimer's, dementia, anything with the head? Did someone have a clot?

Sheri: Not that I can think of.

Terry: Okay. It has to do with the name Mary or Maria. Now. If they don't give me their name, they'll give me the name...

Sheri: My grandmother's name is Marie.

Terry: There you go.

Sheri: My mother's mother.

Terry: Oh. Okay. She's here.

Sheri: Her name was Marie. She was young. She had maybe it was like they thought she was having a heart attack. She could have had a stroke. She could have had a clot. It was before I was born.

Terry: She wants to come in. She doesn't want to miss out, she's saying. She brings in a carousel. So when I see a carousel, someone collects little horses or I go to Connecticut and the reason why you may have a connection to the state of Connecticut is because of the carousel in the Danbury Mall.

Sheri: The only thing I can think of is my mother was from Long Island, Freeport and there was this place that had all like carousels and rides, so maybe it was that. That was years ago when I was little. I remember they had that.

Terry: Okay. So you remember they have to come in with either a memory or a current event.

Sheri: And that's great because I didn't have the pleasure of knowing my grandmother.

Terry: Oh. She knows you. So you know, if they're going to show me something medical, it'll be fine. Okay?

Sheri: Alright.

Terry: "The one living with breast issues, tell her not to worry", this grandmother is saying. Did anybody either find a lump or was there a scare with breast issues?

Sheri: You want to know something? I don't know if this has to do with me because today I go for my mamo and my ultrasound and I've been freaking the frig out.

Terry: So maybe she's trying to tell you it's fine.

Sheri: I've been freaking. I've been going since I was twenty-three. My mother died at thirty-three years old from breast cancer.

Terry: Oh, did she? So it is probably for you.

Sheri: I go at three thirty.

Terry: Three thirty and she was thirty-three. It'll be fine. That's what she's saying. It'll be fine.

Sheri: I've been freaking out. I want to cry. I should be used to this. I'm forty-six. I've been going for twenty-three years. But every year I freak myself out. I was young. I watched what it did to my mother. I watched what it did.

Terry: That poor thing.

Sheri: She was only thirty-one when she got diagnosed. I watched what it did.

Terry: She was a baby.

Sheri: Yeah. So I got cheated from a mother, from a grandmother. Now the sad part is the breast cancer is on my mother's side. My mother was the one and only, and my mother has three sisters.

Terry: I think she's going to remain the one and only. So not to worry about that.

Sheri: Yup. It's got to be me because I'm going today.

Terry: Isn't that funny? So they're very good, your family on the other side. Your father wants me to ask you, "Did you learn your lesson about the food business?"

Sheri: Yes!

Terry: What the hell is he talking about?

Sheri: *Laughs* We had a deli.

Terry: You did?

Sheri: He had a deli. We gave it up. We gave it up two years ago.

Terry: He said, "Did you learn your lesson?"

Sheri: I learned my lesson, yeah.

Terry: Did someone go into the hospital? Let's say you're going to have a procedure done and they mark the spot. Did someone get a mark on the wrong spot?

Sheri: Not as far as I know.

Terry: Alright. Because he's showing me somebody put a mark either on the right side and it should have been on the left and it had to be changed.

Sheri: Wasn't me, thank God. I was the only one there with my knee.

Terry: Keep that in mind because it may happen.

Sheri: Okay.

Terry: But it will be caught, so you don't have to worry about that. No. No. You know it's that blue dot thing or whatever the hell it is.

Sheri: Yeah. Because they mark it. They came in and drew all over me before mine.

Terry: Dad's showing me a talking bird. Who had this bird? This parrot?

Sheri: He did.

Terry: "This fucking bird," he said, "is with me too."

Sheri: But it wasn't a real bird.

Terry: Doesn't matter.

Sheri: He had this thing and he would laugh hysterically. He'd press the button, walk around. He taunted everybody with the frigging bird.

Terry: There you go. So he's doing it now, even on the other side. Having a great time.

Sheri: Holy shit. The remote for that thing he used to walk around with it and laugh hysterically.

Terry: Really? Oh, so he had to be a character.

Sheri: He was a ball buster.

Terry: Okay. He's showing me a new car. Who got a new car?

Sheri: His wife did. She traded in both the cars through him and she got a new car.

Terry: That's what he's showing me because he knows that too. So he's saying to me, "You know it's nice seeing you again. I didn't believe in you the first time".

Sheri: Yup. No.

Terry: That's what he's saying. "I thought you were all nuts, so I wanted to make sure you weren't going to take advantage of them. But then it wasn't that expensive. I figured they could have a good time. They could laugh." But he said, "When you read me, I started thinking it's possible." He was very happy to see Mom. She came and got him right away.

Sheri: Really? Okay. You know, it's funny because he was in Rosary Hill right before he passed. I walked in the room and he looked at me and he goes, "Why does she look so different?" And I moved out of the way and then he goes, "Oh she looks the same". The only thing I could figure is my mother must have walked in with me. I'm identical to my mother, but there are differences. There's a lot. Since he passed my family keeps saying, "Oh my God. You look like your father". And I never looked like my father. But I'm thinking maybe he saw my mom.

Terry: She was there.

Sheri: She's a strong presence. I know my mother's a strong presence. I know my mother has protected me and my brother all these years. I really do feel that.

Terry: Where's the ring?

Sheri: My brother has it.

Terry: Because your mom's doing this. *Pointing to the ring finger* Where's the ring? Why does your brother have it?

Sheri: Because he had gotten kidney cancer from 9/11 years ago, so I gave it to him, but it was with the understanding to hold on to it. It's been since 2013. I haven't got it back and I don't have the heart to say anything about it to him. Because I used to wear it. I would wear her wedding ring.

Terry: So he holds onto that to be close to Mom.

Sheri: He was like this with my mother. *Crosses middle and pointer fingers*

Terry: That's why. You'll get it back. He doesn't have a daughter, does he?

Sheri: No. He has two sons.

Terry: Good. Yeah. So you'll get it back. Did you have an engagement or a wedding in the family?

Sheri: Just recently?

Terry: Well, it's going to be after Dad passed.

Sheri: I'm trying to think if anyone got married after my father passed.

Terry: Or did someone get engaged? Was someone talking about getting engaged?

Sheri: My cousin, Danielle. She got married after my father died.

Terry: Oh, she did. Because Dad was telling me there is a current event with an engagement or a wedding. Do you remember seeing something go right by the corner of your eye?

Sheri: I see stuff all the time.

Terry: That's Dad.

Sheri: Okay.

Terry: So it's not your imagination.

Sheri: I see. I hear. My ears ring. All the time.

Terry: You're starting to become more in tune with the other side. Just know how to protect yourself. Please. He's doing this to something. *Pretends to lift the cover up off of something* Do you have something like to hold blankets in? To me, it looks like a piece of furniture. It could be a toy chest. It has a lid that opens upwards.

Sheri: We have a toy chest. I actually have the toy chest from when me and my brother were little. I gave it to my brother. But I also have a toy chest that my little brother made for my son. That I have.

Terry: You do. And what room is it in?

Sheri: It's downstairs where his picture is.

Terry: There you go. So that's where he is. He's showing me what he sees.

Sheri: And downstairs, where his picture is now, is because my daughter moved back. She's downstairs.

Terry: Oh, he's always down there. The noise in the wall isn't Dad.

Sheri: Okay.

Terry: Have you been hearing...

Sheri: I hear things all the time.

Terry: But it's the noise in the wall. That's not Dad because that would be scary and Dad does not make noise to scare anyone. And when your daughter is down there if he can sense if she gets a little nervous, he leaves. Because he's not there to frighten anyone. But I don't know if it's the pipes in the wall, the wires in the wall. There is something going on, but it's mechanical, not spiritual. He wants me to tell you.

Sheri: Okay.

Terry: Did you write a letter to him?

Sheri: Yes.

Terry: He wants to thank you for that.

Sheri: It wasn't a very nice letter.

Terry: It doesn't matter.

Sheri: It's in my phone. I did it in my phone.

Terry: Because that was real. That's what he's telling me. That is how you feel.

Sheri: I was mad at him. I was mad at him about a lot of things.

Terry: But he's thanking you for that. Because then you get it out of your system. And that you trusted his love enough, believe it or not, that you knew I'm not going to take it personally and it was, believe it or not, very healing for you. So to give it to him so that he could have a last hand in some kind of healing, even though he was responsible for some kind of hurt, it made it full circle for him.

Sheri: There was a lot of hurt growing up.

Terry: He knows about the letter. He read every word.

Sheri: Oh crap.

Terry: And he knows you know that he loves you. Because I asked him telepathically, because you know I don't give messages of love. Unless there was a problem. So I asked, "Should I?" He said, "No. We're good". And then he mentioned the letter. Because you have to love someone to trust them like that. So he called someone an idiot. I'm on either a motorcycle, a dirt bike. This is something I shouldn't be on.

Sheri: It could be my son. And he was like this with my son.

Terry: He's an idiot. What is he doing?

Sheri: Just so happened a couple of weeks ago I was driving by. I was going home past one of my son's friends' houses. They were hanging outside. One of my son's friends was on the dirt bike and I said, "Joey, stay off the frigging thing". "Alright Mom. Alright." So I don't know what he did prior or what he did after I went away.

Terry: Okay. So your father's saying, "Idiot". He must have been there because you can't just pick this shit up. What's wrong with the vacuum? Did you have to get a new vacuum? Because he's making me feel the vacuum isn't working the right way.

Sheri: I don't know. I just got a new one.

Terry: Oh. So you did just get a new one. Good. How long ago did you get a new one?

Sheri: About a month ago.

Terry: Then yes. So then that's cool. You had to replace it because it wasn't working. So your father knew that as well. The clock that's not telling the right time.

Sheri: In my room.

Terry: Your father, that makes him nuts.

Sheri: It's ticking, but it's just not staying with the time. I look at it and I'm like son of a bitch. It's the wrong time.

Terry: Isn't that funny? It drives your father nuts. Also, the renovations. Were you doing renovations or talking about renovations? Am I in the kitchen?

Sheri: We just moved into another house. It's a brand new house.

Terry: How long ago?

Sheri: We only moved there in April.

Terry: So it's relatively new. But there's going to be something. I'm still going to go in the kitchen in that house. So I don't know whether an appliance has to be repaired. There's going to be something. "It's not going to be a major thing, but it is going to be something", he's saying.

Sheri: Okay.

Terry: Dad had a friend on the other side. This man died way before he did, he's telling me. And he knew this gentleman through the fire department.

Sheri: Very well. There very well could have been.

Terry: And how do you know a Jim, Jimmy, James?

Sheri: Jimmy's his brother.

Terry: This guy also knew his brother.

Sheri: Really.

Terry: Don't think about it right now. I don't know how he knew his brother also, but he knew him. Alright, hold on a second. So this is Dad, "You might have been cured of the food business with the deli, but not everyone was convinced". Your father wants me to tell you whether you open a restaurant, even if you work in a deli, you work in a food store, it's always going to be hard work. So there's someone who's not convinced yet. It's always going to be hard work.

Sheri: See, my husband went a totally different direction though now. He's in other businesses now.

Terry: I'm telling you there's still someone in the family, in the back of their mind, they either want to get a restaurant or something. The food business, according to Dad, is always going to be hard.

Sheri: I'm done with that.

Terry: Not Mom, but I have an equal female with Dad. Equal female could be a sister, sister-in-law, friend, cousin.

Sheri: All his sisters are here.

Terry: Nope. Did he have a cousin? I know your name is ███████, but are you Italian?

Sheri: Oh yeah.

Terry: Oh you are?

Sheri: My mother's side is Italian.

Terry: Yeah. Okay. This woman's coming in from your mother's side because what I heard was, you know, it's like with me. You know you're paisans. You don't have to be blood. So I know that's Italian.

Sheri: Could it be, Jane, his second wife is also Italian? Her mother, who I called Grandma because she was my grandma, passed away.

Terry: No. Equal to Dad's generation. So generations are only ten years.

Sheri: Trying to think. All my mother's sisters are here.

Terry: Did she have a cousin that she lost?

Sheri: Jane lost a cousin, Patricia.

Terry: There you go. That's who it is. Okay. She's on the other side. She wants to come in.

Sheri: I was always around them growing up.

Terry: So she wants to say hello. Your mother's allowing it and your mother's showing me Italian, Italian.

Sheri: Okay. My mother's Italian.

Terry: The big tree. Was there a big tree in your backyard? Maybe where you were. This is a thin bark. But did it look half dead? Was there a problem with a tree? Or was it a big fruit tree?

Sheri: Where I am?

Terry: Or where you were because remember, it could be a memory. The kind of tree I'm seeing has small bark.

Sheri: Okay. I'm trying to think. Well, at his house he had all pine trees lining the driveway that looked dead.

Terry: Oh okay. So that's what Dad is showing me. Because they're tall and they're thin.

Sheri: Yes.

Terry: And he was saying, and you'll hear me saying *points to recording device*, did it look dead? Or was it dead? Two-dollar bills. He's handing me two-dollar bills. Who collects two dollar bills? Or do you have a two-dollar bill?

Sheri: I might. I probably do somewhere.

Terry: Alright. Because he's specific about the two-dollar bill. "When you find the two-dollar bill, always have it in your wallet", he's saying, "so you'll always have money. Not to ever spend it, but this way you know." Your mother's saying, "Listen. We're here for you and your brother." They're both extremely happy.

Sheri: Good. I'm having a rough time. I do. I still have a rough time even though it's going on three years. With him and my mom; I lost her when I was nine. I feel slighted. But I'm having a rough time. I feel like an orphan.

Terry: Well, you are. You don't have a mother or father.

Sheri: I went from having a big family - because even my stepmother left - to nothing.

Terry: Well, you have your kids.

Sheri: That's the thing. That's where I have to get myself; that I have my kids and my husband.

Terry: You're the matriarch of your family. And you'll have grandchildren and everything. So you've learned what not to do. According to Dad, I'm only repeating what he's saying, you're blessed with having a lifelong partner where Dad wasn't. So he must have been young also when she passed.

Sheri: My father, yeah. Well, if my mother was thirty-three, he was thirty-four.

Terry: They're still kids. Wait until one of your children turns thirty-four. You're going to see they're still kids. They don't think. They still think about themselves.

Sheri: They had a rocky marriage, my mother and father, they did. They had a rocky marriage. I'm glad they're happy now because they had a rocky marriage.

Terry: They're happy now because we're no longer human on the other side. We're back to being spiritual beings. Also, why is he talking about Pennsylvania now?

Sheri: He used to drive there all the time. He used to drive there all the time to buy cigarettes.

Terry: Get the hell out. So he's asking you to drive to Pennsylvania for the frigging cigarettes.

Sheri: I used to drive there all the time. I quit smoking. He's probably happy. I don't know if they're happy. I quit a year and a half ago.

Terry: Good for you.

Sheri: Yup. He used to drive there all the time, to Pennsylvania.

Terry: Oh. So he was addicted to cigarettes.

Sheri: Oh yeah.

Terry: Chain smoker.

Sheri: Up until the month before he died. Yup. Up until and he was like, "this didn't even kill me".

Terry: And how old was he when he passed?

Sheri: Sixty-eight.

Terry: Oh, so he was only a couple of years older than me, so he was young.

Sheri: In December is his birthday. He turned sixty-eight on December fourteenth. He died January fourth.

Terry: Wow. So he was a young sixty-eight.

Sheri: Yup.

Terry: Wow. Who has the criminal past? So a criminal past could be I had a run in with the cops, maybe I did get arrested, or it could be as simple as getting a speeding ticket because that's a criminal ticket.

Sheri: I don't know. Could be anybody with a speeding ticket.

Terry: Your father's telling me go to - it's a hot car. Did someone back in the day, I don't know, maybe your dad was involved in this?

Sheri: Him. He did some shit, man.

Terry: Okay. Yeah. So he's owning everything that he's doing. And he's still giving me things I would not know. Because these have to be new readings. That's why I tell people if you think you need a new reading, don't call me. That's just you wanting it. But if you feel you need it, that's *them* telling you there are new signs. So it makes my job a lot easier. Are you still unable to make a hard-boiled egg?

Sheri: Me?

Terry: Like it doesn't come out right.

Sheri: They always crack.

Terry: Okay. You still don't know how to do it. Your mother is saying, "Leave her alone". He mentions the name George.

Sheri: That's my maiden name.

Terry: Get the hell out.

Sheri: That was his last name. George.

Terry: This is why I don't think in the reading. I thought his last name was ███████, but that's your husband's name.

Sheri: That's my husband's name. That's my maiden name.

Terry: So your maiden name is George? Oh, isn't that funny? Oh my God. Do you have Mom's mirror?

Sheri: I have a little compact.

Terry: Of hers?

Sheri: Yes.

Terry: Okay. Because that's what she's showing me. Also someone living, acid reflux or we call it agita, but it's heartburn.

Sheri: I have it. My daughter has it.

Terry: You do. Okay. Alright. Because Mom is making me feel burning from here up.

Sheri: I have it. My daughter has it.

Terry: So you and your daughter. This is what Dad does. *Pounds fists together*

Sheri: My middle one. Yeah. She's me.

Terry: And that's what the problem is. She's you. But she'll love you until the day you die. She won't let anyone treat you like she does.

Sheri: No. She won't let anyone treat any of us the way she does. She can say whatever she wants to us, but not anybody else.

Terry: Because she'll step in. But he likes that she's feisty.

Sheri: She's very feisty. She's a little thing, but she's very feisty.

Terry: Is she a little thing?

Sheri: Yup.

Terry: He's glad. I don't know if it's her or the other daughter because I don't know how many kids, but did she get rid of the boyfriend?

Sheri: Well, they both did. Both my daughters.

Terry: Okay. He's happy about that.

Sheri: Okay. The middle one doesn't have a new one. The older one does, and he knew him, but they weren't together when my father was alive.

Terry: There you go. Okay. Good. Is your father-in-law on the other side?

Sheri: Well, yes. I didn't get to know him, but yes. Not the ones that raised my husband, but my mother-in-law and father-in-law are on the other side.

Terry: Because your father's bringing them. He's saying, "Tell her I have her father-in-law".

Sheri: You want to know what's really bad, too? His name was Jack.

Terry: Really?

Sheri: I didn't even think about that. They both died when my husband was seven.

Terry: Oh wow. So you have that in common. But I have his dad here to come in and say hello.

Sheri: Oh wow. That's kind of neat because I didn't get to know them.

Terry: Does he have one picture of them?

Sheri: I have a picture. This is going to sound really bad, but in my bedroom I have like a shrine. It's a cabinet. And it's filled with pictures of my mother, my father, my husband's parents and I have feathers, pennies that I find, anything that I find.

Terry: Did his mom have a miscarriage?

Sheri: My husband's mother? I don't know.

Terry: Because your father-in-law is holding a baby boy. So it has to be a bloodline to him.

Sheri: Really? The sad part is my stepmother had a miscarriage.

Terry: Nope. Has to be blood to him.

Sheri: She could have. I don't even know. It could have been before my husband. I don't even know.

Terry: Okay. Because he is holding this boy and I see it as a boy. And I see it either as a miscarriage. Well back then it would be more miscarriage than abortion.

Sheri: You know one of my husband's cousins lost a son. The baby died after it was born.

Terry: There you go.

Sheri: It would have been his nephew's.

Terry: His blood.

Sheri: Yup.

Terry: He has the baby.

Sheri: Wow.

Terry: He's pointing to the shoulder. Who's having shoulder issues?

Sheri: His son.

Terry: Okay. So he's pretty strong on the other side. And it was because of your dad he wanted to show respect to your husband more so than just asking for him. So he just asked the father to come because the mother was off doing something. I like what your father did today. He made my job easier. Thank you so much. And I thought it was going to be very difficult because I read you before.

Sheri: Yup. Yup. I really felt like I needed to come. I needed it. You know when you just feel like... I felt like I needed it because I spent so much time talking to them and I look for signs. I think they're sending me signs. It's funny. Yesterday or the day before, because I work myself up about my mammography and stuff, I'm driving home and I'm in the car crying and I'm like alright, I've been seeing a lot of feathers and I've been seeing a lot of orange butterflies. I think they're signs. I don't know if they're signs and on my visor in my car I have their funeral cards. I have palm. The palm dropped right into my pocketbook.

Terry: There you go. And what does April have to do with it?

Sheri: April?

Terry: Yeah.

Sheri: I don't know.

Terry: The month of April. What does that have to do with the family?

Sheri: I don't know.

Terry: Okay. That's going to be a big sign because palms are associated with the month of April.

Sheri: Yup.

Terry: So that's not even a coincidence.

Sheri: Dropped right into my pocketbook.

Terry: There you go.

Aha Moment: Sheri reached out to let me know she is expecting a grandchild. The baby is due to be born in April.

A Letter From Sheri

☆ ★ ☆ ★ ☆ ★ ☆ ★

My father, Artie, was the oldest of six. He was born and raised in the Bronx, New York. In the sixties, he met my mother out on Long Island. They married in 1969. They had my older brother and me. We lived in the Bronx. Sadly, in 1982, we lost my mother to breast cancer at the young age of thirty-three.

In 1984, my father remarried and my little brother and sister were born. My father was a master electrician. There wasn't anything he didn't know about electrical work. He taught a lot to my brothers and even my husband. I truly believe he was so proud to pass that on.

What can I say about my father? To know him was to love him. He had a pretty gruff exterior, but personally, I think he was sensitive on the inside. I know he loved all four of us, but he definitely was not the huggy kissy type.

Here are some of my favorite memories of my dad. Christmas by far was my father's favorite holiday. When I was young and we lived in the Bronx, going to see the house on Hollywood Ave was a must. We lived in an apartment, but my parents always had a lot of decorations - from the fake fireplace with the yule log my grandfather made to the door made to look like a present. In the nineties, we all pretty much migrated to Putnam and Dutchess Counties, so now he had a house to decorate. He started decorating in November so Thanksgiving night he could turn those lights on.

My father was also a devout catholic. I have never seen someone so strong in his faith up until he passed away. I will get to that later. My father loved his rather large nativity set for outside. He built a manger and displayed it with pride every year. I am so happy that now I have the set and it will be displayed with the same pride. As I type this, I am crying because whenever I go into a store and all the Christmas decorations are displayed, I just stand there and stare and look at all the lights. I also cry because I know dad won't be here another Christmas.

My father was a very proud grandfather. He was very different as a grandparent than a parent. Those kids didn't really know his tough exterior like we did. At the time of his passing, there were six grandchildren. Those kids did no wrong in his eyes, and I know they all miss him terribly. In the last year, we had two more additions to the family. I feel so bad that my father is not here to watch them grow, but I firmly believe those babies met him before they were born.

Now I will get to the memories I live with every single day; the ten months my father was sick. In April 2016, my father was diagnosed with liver cancer. It was definitely a very large blow to our family. We truly didn't see that coming. I sat with my dad a lot over the next ten months. I knew he was so scared, but when I tell you he stayed so strong in his faith, it was remarkable.

My father said to me one day, "It started with you".

I said, "Dad, what are you talking about?"

Years prior, I was sick and we couldn't figure out what was wrong. Thankfully, it was figured out a few very long years later. My brother and sister also had some things go on. My dad explained that when my siblings and I got sick, he asked God to make us better and give it to him. All my doubts about my father being proud of me or loving me went away at that moment.

I still have visions of watching my dad deteriorate in front of my eyes. When my mom was sick I saw her deteriorate, but didn't understand it. I'm thankful now that I didn't. In October 2016, my father made the decision to spend his final days in Rosary Hill in Hawthorne, New York. I truly believe that he lasted another two and a half months because he was there and the care the staff and the nuns gave to him.

I cannot describe the feeling you get when you walk into that home. Only thing I can say is this feeling of peace comes over you. My father was able to hold on for one final Christmas. The tree they put up there is magnificent. There are nativities in every corner. My father had the honor of meeting Cardinal Dolan while he was there. He was so happy. On Christmas Eve I really saw a change in my dad, not that I didn't notice differences on a daily basis. He didn't engage in conversation anymore. He just stared at the wall in front of his bed. It was a picture of water and sailboats. Everyone had their own idea of what it reminded them of. It reminded me of City Island. We used to visit there quite frequently when I was a child. We had family there. In my mind, it was like being on vacation. You see, I would text my dad when I got home from Rosary Hill. He always answered, even if it was a kissy emoji. He didn't that night.

On December 28th I decided to get up and go to dad quite early. That day is the anniversary of my mother's passing. In the back of my mind, I was so scared that my father would pass away that day as well. I know I probably seem selfish because my father was suffering so much, but I just didn't want him to go that day. Honestly, I didn't think I could handle it. When I got there, he was just staring at the picture again. He then asked me to give him his newspaper. Anyone that knew my father knew he didn't go a day without reading the paper. Dad must've noticed the date. He said to me, "Do you know what day it is?"

I said, "Of course Dad. I already went to church to light candles. I lit some for mommy and for you as well."

He said, "I never want you to forget."

I said, "Don't worry Dad. I never will."

After that, he said, "I'm going to take a nap."

I said, "Okay, I will be here". I think that was actually the last conversation I had with my father where he wasn't in a different year or time.

Dad actually passed away exactly a week later. It was the shortest, but longest week of my life. I believe I watched him go through every year of his life. We watched him have conversations with family that had passed. I thought I wanted to be there when he was taken to heaven, but I couldn't do it. My older brother stayed with him. I give him a lot of credit. My brother doesn't speak about it, only that it was peaceful.

So that's somewhat of the story of my father. He definitely did things his way.

FOUR

☆ ★ ☆ ★ ☆ ★ ☆ ★

Spirituality is fluid. We grow, experience love and pain, and evolve. We shouldn't remain the same person our entire lives because that would mean we haven't developed. It's important to advance ourselves throughout our lifetime and strive to become better than we once were. You may feel a calling to become spiritual or revisit your religion. You may feel a need or want to perform parts of spirituality you haven't tapped into yet - like visiting a church or learning how to meditate. There is no right or wrong way to express your faith, but there are lessons to be learned to make sure you're not inviting the wrong type of energy into your life. The more open you are to the other side, the more open the other side will be to you. Signs are everywhere. Sometimes you just need a lesson on how to read them. Keep learning. Keep trying. And keep yourself open to the other side. The best is yet to come.

☆ ★ ☆ ★ ☆ ★ ☆ ★

∞ The Story of Eight ∞

Amanda's Reading

☆ ★ ☆ ★ ☆ ★ ☆ ★

Terry: So I guess you saw our little whatever it was (Facebook Live) that we did. You know when we got off a lot of people were saying, "Oh my God, you're funny". I asked Dawn, "were we funny"? We had no clue.

★ ☆ ★ **See this Video on Youtube** ☆ ★ ☆

The Thanksgiving Table
with
Spiritual Medium Terry Marotta &
Psychic Medium Dawn Marie

SCAN ME

Amanda: You were very funny.

Terry: Oh my God. We had a good time with it.

Amanda: My Aunt was the one that came through and said, "Shit or get off the pot". So I said alright, I guess it's time for me to get another reading.

Terry: But the other thing that's happening with you is you have spirits around you now.

Amanda: Yeah.

Terry: They don't just belong to you.

Amanda: Yeah.

Terry: Somehow you opened up a portal because when I went into prayer all of the sudden it got cold. Now I read and I deliver messages from those who have passed almost on a daily basis. If I get a cold, that means there's a lot of them coming in at one time and they don't all belong to the same person.

Amanda: That makes sense.

Terry: So, I have all these signs, but we'll go through them in a minute.

Amanda: Okay.

Terry: What did you do or what do you think you did between - you said June you came to see me - and now that could have created the portal?

Amanda: I'm getting chills. I know they're here.

Terry: I know. They're there.

Amanda: I know they are. I opened myself up. I started meditating back at the end of April. During COVID times I needed to destress and a good friend of mine opened herself up. She said, "I know you have abilities and I know that there's a lot kind of holding you down" and she said to meditate. So I basically meditated. I've gotten very much into crystals.

Terry: Good. Okay.

Amanda: I have a lot of those around. I see a lot of Angel numbers. There are a lot of signs and I know I've opened up things. I don't always understand what it is, but I always know its good energy because I feel energies. But I just meditated. That's really it. I really just started to open myself up. I pray. I've become much more spiritual.

Terry: Spiritual is the breath. Religion has to do with the brain and learning facts and you don't really need that.

Amanda: No. I'm not religious by any means. I'm spiritual.

Terry: When you're spiritual, you're actually breathing your beliefs. It's the breath of the body.

Amanda: This year has been a huge year of spiritual growth for me.

Terry: Now so far you've been protected by Archangel Michael.

Amanda: Yes. I pray to him every day.

Terry: Now his name day along with the other archangels is 9/29. That's their name day; the 9/29. Okay?

Amanda: Alright.

Terry: The 1's - repetitive ones - anything two or more, that's Archangel Michael. The 2's, that's Archangel Raphael. He's the healer. The 3's; that's Archangel Gabriel. He's the messenger. He brings messages from the other side. The 4's, because you're going to need to know this, the 4's are Archangel Uriel, who brings the light of God's will. Okay? The 5's, that's Archangel Metatron. He removes any interior barriers you may have that maybe you built up that will keep you away from the light. When you see all nines, that's all the archangels. It's an army of archangels near you.

Amanda: What if you see four 9's?

Terry: That's them.

Amanda: What about 777?

Terry: Seven is a very religious number, believe it or not. Alright.

Amanda: I see it all the time.

Terry: Seven is on your path because, according to what people believe, it took God seven days to create the earth. You know, we have seven days in the week.

Amanda: That makes sense.

Terry: So seven will feed more the religious aspect, not so much the spiritual aspect. And eights is infinity. If you're not a child - which you're not. You're an adult - and you open up the portal, you'll start seeing a lot of eights. I'll always be open then. Now you're going to have to learn how to protect yourself.

Amanda: I see 888. Honestly, I've even seen 666. I've seen every number.

Terry: Okay. So the good part of the 666 is it's just the archangels inverted. Because the movies will make you think 666 is the devil. It's not. Now let's go through what I heard before getting... well *Terry telepathically speaks to the spirits*. Okay. I'll tell her. Hold on a second. You have to start to be able to feel the energies coming. Do I feel them more on my right side or do I feel them more on my left? The right side means those are your loved ones. The left side doesn't make them bad, it's just they're not directly associated with you. So let's say your friend's brother passed and you might feel something over your left shoulder. So you would know then, "I'm going to have to deliver a message for someone". So she knows the brother is okay and all that other good stuff. Alright. The month of November. What does any day in November or the eleventh of any month or the number eleven mean to you?

Amanda: You know, that came up on my last reading as like a fourth month and it didn't dawn on me. That's my anniversary with my husband. We got married in November.

Terry: Let's just leave it there.

Amanda: I had time to think about it.

Terry: The month of August. What does any day in August or the eighth of any month or the number eight? Now, with this number eight, I don't repeat myself. So I'm not speaking about the repetitive eights and its eternity. Maybe someone has six children and made it a family of eight. Or maybe someone had eight kids. Who knows? But does any day in August or the eight any month of the number eight mean anything to you?

Amanda: The only thing about August that was big that happened was my husband's grandfather…

Terry: Passed.

Amanda: … had passed away.

Terry: He's here. He's the one coming through.

Amanda: I know he's here.

When Amanda said this, her audio distorted for a moment. If you're like us and believe there is no such thing as a coincidence, then this was another confirmation from the spirit coming through.

Amanda: He's always with me. I'm telling you, I opened up so much and I feel. I don't always know who's with me, but I sense certain loved ones are near me.

Terry: So what's going to happen to you now? So let me tell you what's happening to me because, as it's happening to me, he's pointing to you. I'm getting digestive issues. Like I feel them. Did this grandfather have digestive problems or does one of his loved ones living have digestive problems?

Amanda: I'm not sure about him and I'm also not sure about his family.

Terry: What about your husband? Or someone in your family?

Amanda: My grandfather has digestive issues.

Terry: Okay, so one grandfather to the other.

Amanda: Yeah.

Terry: Okay. So you're going to start feeling. You're going to become intuitive as well. Because for this grandfather to make me feel like something is wrong with my stomach, it's digestive issues.

Amanda: I've had a lot of digestive issues in the past few weeks. Is that not mine?

Terry: That's not yours. That's him telling you that's him. But here's the difference. They don't last long when they're not yours.

Amanda: Okay. It's intermittent.

Terry: Yes. That's him. I don't know why he chooses that sign, but that's his sign. And the last month is June. What does any day in June or the sixth of any month, the number six... Can I just ask you something before I even finish with that?

Amanda: Yes.

150

Terry: Did he used to whistle? *Terry imitates a short loud whistle.* Who used to whistle?

Amanda: I had a great grandfather that used to whistle a lot.

Terry: Because I'm hearing whistling. And I'm hearing it with these ears. *Points to her ears*

Amanda: Oh yeah. That's him.

Terry: Really? How cool is that? So don't get freaked out if you start hearing the whistle.

Amanda: He didn't come through the last reading.

Terry: What happened?

Amanda: Last time we met, he didn't come through and I was surprised he didn't come through. I said to him afterwards, in my head, I said I can't believe you didn't come through. I wanted him to come in tonight. That's him.

Terry: Yeah. By the whistle. Now let me tell you with the whistle. It sounds like a regular whistle. But it also sounds far away. Even though I hear it in my ear, it sounds far away. So it's weird. The first time it happens to you, you'll know what I'm speaking about because the words are limiting the actions. It's like I hear it, but I know it's far away. Let's go back to June. So either any day in June, the sixth of any month, or the name Anthony or Tony. I go to that name because for me this is Saint Anthony's month. So does any day in June or anything else mean something to you?

Amanda: The only thing and I don't remember; was our first reading in June?

Terry: No. Not going there.

Amanda: Oh. My grandmother. My grandmother died in June. Duh. My grandmother. That's what it is.

Terry: There you go. She put cards out on the table in front of me.

Amanda: Oh yeah.

Terry: Okay. That makes sense to you. Why?

Amanda: She used to play cards. When she was younger, she would go out with friends and play cards.

Terry: There you go. So she's still doing that. How do you know the names Nick, Nicky, Nicolas or Nicole?

Amanda: Nick is a husband. We know him. He's not related to me. He's someone who my dad and his wife grew up with. That's her husband. That's the only Nick that I can think of.

Terry: Not going there. I don't feel it.

Amanda: They're friends of my family.

Terry: Does your husband have - because remember, you'll bring his energy in here as well. Especially if November is the anniversary of the wedding of you and your husband. Is it someone at work? A neighbor?

Amanda: My husband has a cousin Nick.

Terry: Okay. Hold on a second. I don't want you to use your brain. Was he just, or were you or your husband just talking about him or talking to him?

Amanda: We talked about him today.

Terry: Okay. So these grandparents who came in, they're giving me a time reference for how long they've been with you. So they were there with you during that conversation. That's why I don't want you to fit it in. The minute you use your brain, you know you're going to create an "Aha" moment.

Amanda: It turns it off.

Terry: It does. You want it to flow. Now this is weird that they're showing me this. So I see you in the shower. I don't see you naked. I see you in the shower getting inspiration when it comes to spirituality or getting answers to questions. Now I have to tell you why it happens in the shower.

Amanda: Okay.

Terry: The water is a purifier and they need electricity. Running water has some kind of currency to it. It's almost like a baptism all over again. So even the shower for me, and they're liking you to me a lot tonight, so for my books, it's when I take a shower they give me the title of the book, they give me the premise of the book. I'm just looking up. The rest of the world does not exist except me and the shower. And that's when they can get to me.

Amanda: Okay.

Terry: Do you have a picture of a grandparent in a military hat? An old, old picture.

Amanda: Yes I do. I'm getting crazy chills.
Amanda's audio distorts again

Terry: Who is that?

Amanda: It was another grandfather.

Terry: On the other side.

Amanda: My dad's dad. Yup.

Terry: Wow. You're calling all these grandparents and it's funny because my rule is after a certain age we figure at least one grandparent is on the other side. So I don't say, "well, I see a grandfather here or a grandmother". They have to prove it to me. And then I'll let them come in. I don't want to totally negate them either, you know? Are you keeping a diary of sorts?

Amanda: Yes.

Terry: But I don't mean writing a list.

Amanda: No, I mean like anything spiritual that happens to me, I write down.

Terry: What you need to do is use a dedicated writing implement. You can't switch off because the writing implement will hold on to the energy. So you do not use it for any other reason but that. And then once it runs out of ink or they really would prefer you do it in pencil.

Amanda: Okay. I'll get a pencil.

Terry: Get a pencil. It'll last longer anyway. You just write a little. Who was the drinker? And I'm on the other side. I'm not living.

Amanda: An uncle.

Terry: On the other side.

Amanda: Yes. On the other side.

Terry: Okay. The drinker is coming through as well. Was he related to Dad?

Amanda: Yes. He was married in.

Terry: He's related. He's your uncle through Dad. He's apologizing to you. And your father's still with us. Correct?

Amanda: Yes.

Terry: Alright. Because he's apologizing to him.

Amanda: To my dad or to me?

Terry: To your dad. And it could have been because you're his daughter, or maybe he never owned up to something, but he's apologizing to your father. Because he has to go up the line first. So whatever he might have done that maybe you considered abusive, he has to go to the father for forgiveness.

Amanda: Interesting. Okay. That makes sense.

Terry: Does it? Alright. How do you know the name Bob, Bobby, Rob, Robby, Robert, or last name Robertson or something like that?

Amanda: Bobby was a grandfather that passed. That's the only Bobby I know.

Terry: That's fine. He wants to be acknowledged. And how do you know the name Vin, Vinny, Vincent, Victor? I'm on the other side as well. Was someone's middle name like Michael Vincent or Anthony Vincent?

Amanda: I'm thinking. I can't think of anyone right now.

Terry: Alright. Let it be an "Aha" moment.

Aha Moment: After the reading Amanda figured out that her father-in-law's friend Vinny passed a few weeks prior to her reading.

Terry: Okay. Is it Dad suffering with the lower back?

Amada: No.

Terry: Who - living - is suffering with the lower back? Not the upper back. Now lower back for me, because my kidneys are in the wrong place, so it could be lower back or it could be kidney issues, UTI issues. I know I'm living because I don't know the gender of that person.

Amanda: Kidney issues could be my sister-in-law.

Terry: Living?

Amanda: Yes.

Terry: Okay. So the good news is….

Amanda: I also have bladder issues, so it could be either one of us.

Terry: Well, let me ask you something. Is the pain for the bladder in the back?

Amanda: No.

Terry: Then no. It's not you. They wrote "G A" on my paper. So I want to show you this archangel because you're going to have to use one of him. This is Archangel Metatron. *Terry points to a statue* You see, this is how he connects the world. He helps you recognize the feelings you're feeling when it comes to spiritual, not physical, but an intuitive feeling. He helps you make sense of images being sent to you. So Archangel Michael will protect, but Metatron, he's the one that helps you between both worlds.

Amanda: That's what I need help with.

Terry: That's what he's making me feel. You can buy him on Amazon.com.

Amanda: Okay.

Terry: Because this one came from Amazon. The thing that you need to do, this is not for religious meaning, but it creates the balance. All the archangels wear rosaries. You can buy those from Amazon.com as well.

Amanda: I have a rosary. Can I put the one I have on?

Terry: That's beautiful. Alright. Because then Archangel Metatron will connect both worlds through the rosary as well.

Amanda: Okay. That's helpful. Thank you.

Terry: You're welcome. Okay. So "G A". Either someone's initials are "G A" or "A G" or the name George, believe it or not. So if it's not George, it could be Lake George. Is there a memory there? Was someone just speaking about it? Was someone just speaking about Georgia?

Amanda: No.

Terry: Does the name George mean something to you?

Amanda: Not at the moment.

Terry: Do the initials "G A" or "A G" mean something to you?

Amanda: I just think of Grandma when I do that. But, no. To me, I don't know. I'm not sure of George.

Terry: Okay, so hold on a second. You ready? Because you have a gut feeling. They're going to speak to you through your gut right now. They're using my mediumship, not yours. Every medium is psychic, but not every psychic is a medium. You're more medium. You may get great intuitions about someone like I just have a feeling you're not going to get that job or I just have a feeling, but that's not your strength. I don't do psychic at all. That's what Dawn is for. Remember Dawn? Half of the comedy team, I guess. You know we got a lot of people that were like, "Thank you. You guys were so funny". Not, "Thank you for bringing in my loved ones". It was confusing. And this grandmother is on the other side, correct?

Amanda: Yes.

Terry: Was this the grandmother that said shit or get off the pot?

Amanda: No, that was her sister.

Terry: Alright. That's fine. They're bringing me to that point. To that shit or get off the pot. You don't have to give me details, but I need some kind of confirmation as to what they're speaking about.

Amanda: Does it have to be for me or could it be for a family member?

Terry: It could be for a family member. Any energy connected to you. Is someone going out with someone they haven't asked them to get married yet?

Amanda: No. My brother-in-law and his girlfriend have been together for a long time. They're supposed to move in together. I have an idea of who it could be for. It's a personal issue, but I have a feeling.

Terry: That's fine. Well, the answer is, shit or get off the pot. Alright? I don't need to know anything else. That's it. Does your house number have an eight in it? In the address.

Amanda: No.

Terry: Okay. Because if it doesn't, that might not be your forever home.

Amanda: I don't think it is. This is a temporary home.

Terry: Okay. Cool. Because they're showing me the number eight as in eternity and if you don't have it in your address, that's not your forever home. So don't get too attached to this.

Amanda: Okay. That makes sense.

Terry: How many children do you have right now?

Amanda: I don't have any. I have two little nieces that I'm very close to, but I don't have any of my own.

Terry: Oh. You're supposed to have three of them.

Amanda: You said that last time. I'm waiting for them.

Terry: But you're welcoming.

Amanda: My husband and I have been trying the whole year. We are very welcoming. They just, it's not the time, I guess.

Terry: Okay. Here's the thing. Again, it's going to sound religious, but it's not. Saint Gerard and Saint Ann are the patron saints of babies. So it's the energy attached to the saint. I'm not telling you to become dedicated to them. But it's almost like a lot of people will pray to Saint Anthony if they lost something. But they limit his abilities. It's not just lost items. It's I lost the ability to sleep. Or I lost the ability to feel secure. Because he's a miracle worker. He's one of two miracle workers. These were jobs that were given to them on the other side. This was their gift when they were here. So like, for me I guess, I'll be doing mediumships between people that have passed and people who are living then. It'll probably be reversed for me. Saint Gerard and Saint Ann. And you pray by the heart because I don't believe in formal prayers because you don't feel the formal prayers. You memorize them and that has nothing to do with anything. So where do you live?

Amanda: In New York. West Harrison.

Terry: Alright. So there's a relic that I have access to. It's actually Saint Gerard's bones that go around the world. Women take it and they rub their belly with it. You can't open the thing. You have to keep it in its little shrine and just say the prayer. So when you get a gut feeling that you may want that, then you just let me know. Do twins run in the family?

Amanda: I don't know on my husband's side. Not on my side.

Terry: Either these two are going to come together or close apart and I see one boy and one girl right now. Like boom, boom.

Amanda: Sounds good to me.

Terry: They want to go to the month of May. What does any day in May or the fifth of any month, the number five, which might be the total number in your immediate family: you, your husband and three kids, but that's not where they're going now - or the name Mary or Maria. So Mary or Maria could be part of a name like Annemarie, Maryann.

Amanda: Oh my God. So my ex's mother, her birthday was on November fifth and her name was Maria.

Terry: Is she on the other side?

Amanda: I don't know. I don't think so.

Terry: Okay. I'm not going to her then.

Amanda: Okay. Good. May? Um. My great grandmother died in May. I don't remember what date, but I know it was May.

Terry: It doesn't matter. It could be any day in May. So did we acknowledge her before this?

Amanda: No. We didn't.

Terry: Okay. So that's how she comes in. And she's saying remember the grandparents. Also, what is it with the Asians? She's showing me, they look Asian to me. So when I see Asians it could be Filipino, Japanese, Chinese, whatever. Do you have any artifacts from them? Like anything that would have an Asian background attached to it.

Amanda: My husband's grandfather, who is on the other side, when we moved in he had given us, I don't know, they were two little Chinese people figurines.

Terry: There you go. You don't know where they are.

Amanda: They're at my father-in-law's house. *audio distorts again*

Terry: Alright, well, he doesn't like that idea. He got them for you. He's saying, "Well, you could at least hide them in your own closet".

Amanda: Alright. I've got to get them.

Terry: Yes, please. Because he's bringing in the Asians.

Amanda: My father-in-law was like, no, don't take those to your new apartment.

Terry: So put them in a shoebox. Put them somewhere.

Amanda: Alright. I need them. Okay.

Terry: I don't know. They bring up all this kind of stuff for me. Who is left-handed or known as lefty?

Amanda: My dad is left-handed.

Terry: Okay. I have an equal male coming in. Equal just means the same generation. Generation is usually ten to fifteen years. Either way. So with Dad. Did he lose a brother, brother-in-law, friend, cousin?

Amanda: He lost his cousin. She was a female. Her husband is the one that came in before. The drinker.

Terry: Oh really? Okay. So he wants to get my attention. Okay. Dad's dad is on the other side.

Amanda: Yes.

Terry: Because I keep hearing him saying, "I'm his dad". Was dad supposed to repair something? He's trying to put a hammer in his hands. So if I'm trying to put a hammer in someone's hands, either they have to repair something. Maybe that is his line of work that he would use a hammer. What's with the hammer? Was he talking about maybe repairing a deck or doing something in the house or outside the house? Maybe a shed?

Amanda: I don't know. There are always little things that have to go on. I can't think of anything right now.

Terry: Okay. I'm going to tell you what the movie is that they're showing me. They're showing me a leak behind the wall. And what's going to happen is it might have to be the sheetrock or something has to be cut out and then repaired. But the leak will not be tremendous. They never show me bad, anyway.

Amanda: Okay.

Aha Moment: After the reading Amanda sent me a message:

"We went on vacation and came home to what felt like a waterbed in our bathtub. It was coming through the wall caulking so we had them come and drain it. We were nervous about it, afraid there was water damage and mold, and it would cost us thousands, but it ended up not being bad."

Terry: Why are they mentioning New Rochelle? Are you associated with New Rochelle at all?

Amanda: My husband works in New Rochelle.

Terry: There you go. So they want to pay attention to him and show him respect. How long are you married?

Amanda: Two years.

Terry: Okay. But you've known him a long time before?

Amanda: Not too long. We're just going on five years of dating each other.

Terry: Alright. Five years is a long time, but when you first met, either there was a feeling of comfort, like you already knew him or you were comfortable with him, because he's a soulmate of yours. Or it was a coincidence how we met. So it's one or the other and that denotes a soulmate.

Amanda: We were talking yesterday about how we met and when I first saw his picture I had a feeling. I had this gut intuition. I felt like I knew him already.

Terry: Wow. Isn't that funny?

Amanda: Yup. After years of praying for him, not knowing that it was him, but just praying for my soulmate to come through. I had that gut feeling.

Terry: Okay. That's why they wanted me to show you. They're playing that movie in my head like you meet and you see each other and you know. Like it makes no sense. Whereas I might have been a little cautious. Normally I would have been cautious, but I don't know. But this was head on.

Amanda: Oh. Totally.

Terry: Who's Rocky? Or the name Rock. Am I an animal?

Amanda: No. Joe has his dad's cousin, named Rocky. But he's still here, though.

Terry: Yeah. That's fine.

Amanda: You know what? It could be his grandfather's brother-in-law who's on the other side. I think his name might have been Rocco.

Terry: Okay. I can go to a Rocco because that's the same name. Rock, Rocky, Rocco.

Amanda: I don't know off the top of my head. I don't know that family very well.

Terry: Is there a Michael in that family as well?

Amanda: Yes.

Terry: Okay, then that's the family I'm going to. And it's more visitation by the way. It's more like they just want to visit. They're just telling me that's who they visit. You tried saging on your own.

Amanda: I tried.

Terry: You fucked it up. In plain English.

Amanda: Uh oh. Okay. How do I fix it?

Terry: Did I send you… I usually send out… How many floors do you have?

Amanda: I have one.

Terry: Oh the one floor. Did you open up every door? Every window?

Amanda: No. I did not open up the windows.

Terry: You have to. Now you kept them in there. They had nowhere to go. However, I will say so here's the thing. I will say because I know you have nothing heavy near you, but you have a lot of traffic in there. So sometimes it can become bothersome. You know at first it's nice, like who's here? Let me know. But then when it starts interfering with your normal life or your earthly life, it's not that much fun anymore. It's like, oh my God, we're all stuck in because of this frigging COVID. I just want to go to the mall. I just want to go to the mall. I want to hear the music. I want to see the people. I want that energy. But if they told you that's where you have to live from now on, that's when it becomes a hell. Even though it's not bad. That's exactly what you're creating now in your home. Exactly. So you don't want to do that.

Amanda: Okay.

Terry: And many people make a mistake when they buy a new house, so keep this in mind. They just want to go and sage it to make sure. If they don't do it correctly, that's like the alarm saying, "This house accepts visitors".

Amanda: Uh oh.

Terry: You don't burn sage for the fun of it. Or some people will just burn sage because they like the smell of it, not realizing what it's doing. First of all, I think sage smells like pot, for me. Like good pot. You know, like a smelly skunk. But just like crystals have functions, sage is not just an innocent incense. It has a job to do and if you don't let it do it the right way; the reverse is going to happen. Okay. They're putting school near you. So when someone puts the energy of school, either you live right by a school, someone works in a school in any capacity, or someone has to take a test either for a new license or certification.

Amanda: I'm a teacher.

Terry: Oh you are. There you go. Who's Ed, Eddie, Edwin, Edmin. I hear Ed. Living. Not passed. And I think I'm a young kid, to be honest with you.

Amanda: I had an Eddie last year in my class.

Terry: Did you get a feeling about him? Or was he behind to you?

Amanda: Well, he was a kid that - I work with special needs and he was in an accident. He had a traumatic brain injury. There's some up here, but he just can't communicate it.

Terry: Did he ever look at you with pleading eyes? Like, help me. Not academically. I'm not feeling academically.

Amanda: Uh huh. Right.

Terry: Because I don't feel that the home life was the best for him.

Amanda: He lives in the center now because he's wheelchair bound, but his home life was definitely not the best.

Terry: There you go. As much as a brain injury that he had because, remember, the brain has nothing to do with the other side. Nothing. That kid's spiritual. He knows stuff. He knows you know stuff. In his mind, he was having a conversation with you through the eyes. Now, is he - well, I don't even know if schools are open anymore - but, if the schools were open, would he be part of that school still?

Amanda: Yes.

Terry: Are you allowed to look in at other children or no?

Amanda: Right now, no.

Terry: Because of COVID.

Amanda: Yes. But before that, yes.

Terry: Just to say hello. Maybe if you see him walking in the hall or something, when things go away, just go out of your way so he has some sense of consistency which is going to be very, very important to him. And he knows you have that light energy.

Amanda: Okay. That sounds okay.

Terry: Who's Joe, Joey, Joseph, Josephine?

Amanda: There's a lot of them. My husband's Joe.

Terry: That's fine. That's all I want to go to. Now I have an equal male coming in for him. So this guy passed young. With Joe in mind, did he have a friend that passed?

Amanda: Not that I know of.

Terry: And the friend used to have a motorcycle or an ATV, like a two-wheeler kind of thing. And I had darker colored hair. Just keep that.

Amanda: I would have to ask him.

Aha Moment: After the reading Amanda figured out her Uncle Joe had a friend named Bobby who had a motorcycle, dark hair and passed from a heart attack in his late thirties.

Terry: Who had the diabetes? Or is someone…

Amanda: Prediabetic?

Terry: Yes. Who's this?

Amanda: It's me. I'm prediabetic.

Terry: Alright. And you're sticking to whatever you have to do. The diet and everything.

Amanda: Yes.

Terry: Alright. Here's the good news for you. They mentioned it. So it'll be okay. It won't interfere with the pregnancy. So now remember I'm a grandmother, and I'm sixty-six so I could be your mother, whatever. Did you have to go in for a scraping or a cleaning out of something?

Amanda: I had to go to a fertility doctor for tests. They went up in there.

Terry: Did they say anything?

Amanda: No. Everything looked normal.

Terry: Okay. They're showing me like a soda bottle without its cap on and all you had to do was put the cap back on and it's fine. It's like an easy fix. This is an easy fix. When did you go to the fertility doctor?

Amanda: In September. Early October.

Terry: Twenty-twenty.

Amanda: Yes. Recently.

Terry. We'll leave like that because this easy fix could be as simple as eliminating something from the diet, adding something to the diet. It's an easy fix because I see you with three children.

Amanda: It's an easy fix?

Terry: Yeah. I hear, "Easy fix".

Amanda: I want to know what it is. Damn it.

Terry: For them not to show me specifically, there's a reason behind everything that they do.

Amanda: I wanted to know if I was right. Because there's something in my mind and I kept telling them, am I right? Am I right?

Terry: You have to have faith. They won't do that with me. That's a psychic thing. I'm not doing psychic. That brings you into tomorrow. So we get what we need. Not what we want. But a reading will get you what you need.

Amanda: Right.

Terry: So just keep that in mind. And then I promised God, whomever that is, anyone I read, I would ask them when they find themselves totally alone to offer up four very informal prayers for four people living. They pray for us. We're close to hell. You can see it becomes clearer and clearer every single day. Four people living: someone you care about, someone you don't know because we have lost souls here or someone you do know who is a lost soul, someone you don't like or trust - the prayer for that one goes, you know what God let them find their way and keep them away from me. And for us to stop killing our kids because we're killing and abusing our kids. They put a fireman here, in a firehouse.

Amanda: Okay.

Terry: I don't know why. That's going to be something when you're dealing with the other side. Keep in mind they're a mirror image from us. So when we're here, we'll ask a question. We want an answer. But the mirror image is they give us the answer and we have to figure out the question. Your answer is it's a fireman and I see the firehouse.

Amanda: Okay.

Terry: They'll bring it to you at the right time.

Aha Moment: After the reading Amanda let me know that she figured out what the fireman and firehouse meant.

"A couple of months prior to the reading, our carbon monoxide detector started to go off. My husband changed the batteries, figuring that was why, and it stopped for a day or so, then started doing it again. We changed the batteries, and it kept doing it. We were a little concerned. I told my husband either there is carbon monoxide, which I doubted, or the spirits are setting it off. As usual, my husband thought I was nuts. So we called the local fire department and asked them to just send someone over just to see if there was a reading. To our surprise, the entire fire department came. Two fire trucks, an ambulance, and police cars. They blocked off our street, came in with axes and were ready to bust down our wall. The entire block was looking at us. Meanwhile, there was no carbon monoxide. They couldn't figure out what was triggering it. To me, it was clear it was the spirits."

A Letter From Amanda

☆ ★ ☆ ★ ☆ ★ ☆ ★

Hi Terry,

I hope all is going well. I had to reach out to you and personally thank you for the messages you gave me during our last reading.

The other side had mentioned in my last reading someone living with pains, bladder, kidney etc. Turns out it was me. It just hadn't happened yet.

About four weeks after our reading, I started having horrible bladder spasms and urgency, with tons of pain. I was up all night, barely eating and drinking only water. I had a bunch of tests run and everything with my bladder appeared "normal." So the doctor told me to go to my fertility doc.

Also during the reading they were saying GA or AG. And they showed you a scraping. Well, guess what? I went to my fertility doc, Alexis Greene (AG) and had a laparoscopy yesterday. They found stage 2 endometriosis which we caught early, thank God, and cleared that out and a bilateral uterus, which was an "easy fix" as per the words of the doctor, also the words you relayed during the reading.

I have to thank you so much because I knew everything was going to be okay. The fact that they mentioned it and you always say if they mention it, it's going to be okay, for me, got me through this very difficult time. I wasn't nervous but oddly enough, excited to have the surgery because I knew this was the end of that chapter.

I was hoping that I can bother you for the relic with Saint Gerard's bones. Now that everything is fixed, I feel more ready than ever to bring these children down into this world. If it's still available and if I can use it, that would be a blessing.

Thanks again for everything!

Sincerely,

Amanda

FIVE

☆ ★ ☆ ★ ☆ ★ ☆ ★

When our loved ones pass over, they constantly watch
out for us, often stopping by in dreams or giving us
gut feelings to help guide us in our everyday lives.
Unfortunately, many of us don't understand how to
read signs and ignore our gut feelings. Never take a
dream of your loved one for granted, especially if
you use any of your primary senses in it, like smell
and touch. Those dreams are actually visits from
your loved one, who may stop by to help you with
something. Sometimes they may be pushing you to
get a reading, even though you've had one before.
Go with your gut. They may be telling you there are
new signs to be read.

☆ ★ ☆ ★ ☆ ★ ☆ ★

∞ The Story of Eight ∞

Diana and Adriana's Reading

☆ ★ ☆ ★ ☆ ★ ☆ ★

Terry: Diana.

Diana: Yes.

Terry: Pencils. I'm going to start reading now. Is that okay?

Diana: Mm hmm.

Terry: I love when I don't have to explain how I work. Just rub the pencil then you're going to hand it off to your sister.

Diana: Okay.

Terry: You were from the Bronx, right?

Diana: Yeah. Took us a little while, but we felt that it was time.

Terry: Wow. I stopped doing the Bronx because I couldn't do the Hutch. By the time I got off the Hutch I was cursing everybody. I'm not in the light.

Okay, for the sake of the recording when you guys started coming up the stairs I felt Mom. Mom's, like I said, she's not annoyed. She could be reflecting the energy that's happening here because when you're on the other side you really don't have any heavy or negative feelings.

Diana: Right.

Terry: But even if they come to us through a dream and they seem sad or something they're just reflecting someone else's energy.

Diana: Yes

Terry: I go beyond frustrated though with this mother. There's a situation going on now. She's beyond frustrated and she thinks you should just lop it off. So what is she speaking of? Is there a problem in the family?

Diana: Yes.

Terry: Okay. Because you're becoming overwhelmed with it.

Diana: Yes.

Terry: And that's what she means by lop it off. She doesn't really mean never talk to this person again; it's stop with the bullshit. Why are you letting it enter your life? You can not fix it. "You understand", she's saying. One of you will get sick over this. The other one doesn't give a shit. So you might be the one who can get sick over it and you're the one that doesn't give a shit.

Adriana: Absolutely.

Diana: Absolutely. She knows us very well, Mom.

Terry: Yeah. "You're her babies", she's saying. You're her babies. She is holding a baby. Isn't that funny? Did someone lose this? It has to be her bloodline. If she's holding it it has to be her bloodline. Why is she holding this baby? Did someone lose a baby? Is someone pregnant? Did she send someone a baby? What's with this baby? "One of you knows and one of you isn't saying it", she's saying. Because this is like a therapy session so I can't and I don't. I don't want people knowing my business. Can I get a confirmation for the baby?

Diana: Yes. Mom said it was my baby.

Terry: Okay. That's why. So she's just confirming that's all. So she's still with the baby. Isn't that funny? Who's having shoulder problems?

Diana: Me.

Terry: Okay. "It's just a nagging kind of thing", she's saying. But you don't have to ice it or anything, but just watch it because you're doing something that aggravates it, she's saying. Okay?

Diana: Mm hmm.

Terry: Okay. Let's go to my months. The month of May. Now, let me tell you what it might mean. It could mean any day in May, the fifth of any month, the number five, the name Mary or Maria. So Mary or Maria could be Annmarie, Maryann. It could be a first or middle. Why is she telling me to go to May?

Adriana: That could be two different things.

Terry: Well it can be and it saves her time.

Adriana: So we know Marie.

Terry: Okay. Who's Marie to her?

Adriana: My father's sister

Terry: Living.

Adriana: She's living.

Terry: Okay.

Adriana: We know a Maria.

Terry: Yeah. I don't feel that.

Adriana: She passed away on the fifth.

Terry: Nope.

Adriana: So it's Marie.

Terry: Yeah. Because she's pointing here. This is living *points to the right side of the table*. This is past *points to the left side of the table*.

Diana: Okay.

Terry: She went to visit Marie. Yeah I know that's going to surprise you. "Because knowledge is like putting a suit of armor on", she's saying. So if she were here in body form she would have checked out that situation herself anyway.

Diana: Right.

Adriana: Yes. She would have.

Terry: Is that part of the problem that's going on in the family?

Adriana: No.

Terry: Okay. Because she makes me feel that this is going to be a little upset and then it goes. It goes away.

Adriana: We haven't spoken to her.

Terry: Oh. So it's not going to be a coincidence when you hear something about her.

Diana: No.

Terry: Because there's no such thing as a coincidence.

Diana: Right.

Terry: Is Dad dating?

Diana: No!

Adriana: No.

Terry: Okay. How long ago did Mom pass?

Adriana: Almost a year.

Terry: She's saying, he's not doing it now. "He's not lying to you about that so relax", she's saying.

Diana: Okay.

Terry: I'm just repeating what Mom says. Okay?

Diana: Uh huh.

Terry: You can't expect him not to. She is his soulmate.

Diana: Absolutely.

Terry: He knows that. He does know it. Maybe he doesn't show it to you girls and maybe you think he's not mourning the way that he should be mourning, but she's saying, "You know how guys are".

Diana: Right.

Adriana: Yes.

Terry: Okay. When the time comes for - and she puts a lot of this near him, by the way. When the time comes for him to pass, whenever it is, Mom is going to be the one. So she doesn't really care.

Adriana: Of course.

Terry: Because keep in mind the time is different on that side then it is on this side.

Diana: Okay.

Terry: So two minutes there, they forget, is like maybe fifty years here.

Diana. Wow.

Terry: So for her it's only two minutes. How serious can it get?

Diana: Right. Right.

Terry: Is she in the cemetery?

Diana: Yes.

Terry: Okay. What's wrong with the headstone? Is it tilting? Was there a problem near the headstone?

Diana: No. She's actually in the wall.

Terry: Okay. There's something wrong. In that area there's something wrong with, not hers in particular, but near her.

Adriana: We haven't gone.

Diana: Right.

Terry: Okay. So when you do. You don't have to because she hates the cemetery.

Adriana: That's why we haven't gone.

Diana: Good.

Terry: Because the cemeteries are for us. She likes talking to you in the house.

Adriana: I agree.

Diana: Yeah she does.

Terry: She hasn't spent one night at the cemetery. She wants you to know that.

Diana: Aw.

Terry: Not one night.

Adriana: Well, she shouldn't.

Terry: She knows it takes a lot of fortitude for you girls not to go there.

Diana: Aw.

Terry: It's going against your grain not to go there.

Diana: Yes. Yes. She's right about that.

Terry: Okay. I know you're in the Bronx, but she's going up north though. Is she in Saint Raymond's cemetery?

Diana: Yes.

Terry: Who's in a cemetery up north? Like she goes, have you ever heard of a cemetery called Gates of Heaven in Hawthorne?

Adriana: I've heard of it.

Diana: I've heard of it. I've heard the name.

Terry: She actually, it's so funny because she makes me feel it's an equal female to her that she actually, not that they visit, but that's their meeting point is near the Gate of Heaven.

Adriana: Wow.

Terry: So with mom in mind, did she lose a friend?

Diana: Yes.

Terry: Okay.

Diana: I'm thinking of Maria.

Adriana: Yeah. Maria.

Terry: Okay. So who's Maria? Oh, so it was a friend of hers.

Diana: It was one of her best friends years ago.

Terry: Okay so don't ask me why they meet up there and then they just take off. She likes walking through walls. Your mother can just walk through a wall. She loves that. Okay. The month of August. What does any day in August, the eighth of any month or the number eight mean to someone. Number eight can mean maybe someone had six children and made it a family of eight or does any day in August mean something to you? This is going to be an "Aha" moment.

Diana: I don't know. I'm drawing a blank.

Terry: Did something happen this past August?

Diana: No. Not that I can think of.

Terry: Okay. That's your "Aha" moment. Don't think about it too much.

Diana: Okay.

Terry: Did someone have five children, maybe they lost a child? That's where she's going.

Diana: Me.

Terry: Okay.

Diana: That's what Mom says. Mom says it was me.

Adriana: Three children. Not five.

Diana: Three, but a family of five.

Terry: Oh it could be a family of five, but I lost one, right?

Diana: Yeah. I mean...

Terry: Okay. It has something to do with you honey - the August.

Diana: She did say that. She did say that the last time. And I did lose a baby even though I didn't know.

Adriana: She didn't know.

Terry: But what is August then? She's saying, "Put the August near her".

Diana: Okay.

Terry: So did something happen in August around you?

Diana. Not that I can think of right now.

Terry: Okay. You might have the answer for her. Not now.

Adriana: That might have been the baby's due date?

Terry: No. Okay. Last month - November. What does any day in November, the eleventh of any month or the number one one.

Adriana: I remember last time about the one one. We see the one one's a lot.

Terry: Oh. So that's what she's showing me.

Dama: We see the one one.

Diana: A lot.

Terry: Alright so that's mom.

Adriana: We see the one one a lot.

Diana: One eleven a lot. Eleven.

Terry: And that's also Archangel Michael by the way.

Adriana: Yes.

Terry: Just so you know. Was it Mom who had problems with her hands?

Diana: From the chemo, she did.

Terry: Okay. Because my hands started hurting me.

Diana: It was one of the side effects.

Terry: Oh it was. Sorry. Someone who was a sheep in wolf's clothing. Was there a woman around you guys that maybe appeared to be trying to help? Maybe turned her back? Why is she saying, "the sheep in wolf's clothing"? This is for someone living.

Diana: I think I know who that is.

Terry: Okay. Like in the beginning you think it's nice and it's not.

Diana: We've been having a lot of issues with her lately.

Terry: Okay. So is this the situation Mom was trying to speak about?

Diana: Yes. Well, it's part of it, but there's also another situation. There's a couple situations.

Terry: This is more frustrating than anything.

Diana: Then it's not this one. It's probably the other situation.

Terry: That's what I mean. The one that you just spoke about. Because you said there's another situation. So your mother put more frustration into that situation than the other. Because the energy is there, but all black. She puts black there.

Diana: Mm hmm.

Terry: She goes to the female Tina. Who's this?

Adriana: We know a Tina.

Diana: Yes.

Terry: Okay. Does she help you out?

Diana: She's a neighbor, but she's actually a friend of the family. We've known her a long time.

Terry: Okay. She puts a little craziness.

Diana: *Laughs* Oh yeah. She's definitely crazy.

Adriana: Yes.

Terry: This, according to Mom, please, okay. This is a good place to visit if you want to laugh, but not to stay there.

Diana: Oh yeah.

Adriana: I agree.

Terry: Meaning nice person, but after that you're going to see the craziness.

Diana: She lives on my block. Its, "Hi. Bye".

Adriana: I thought she happens to be like a childhood friend of our mom.

Terry: And that's okay. So you respect her by saying hi and then bye. Not that she would ever harm you girls. That's not what your mother is saying. But she's a little, um, crazy. I'm just going to put crazy.

Diana: Exactly. That's her.

Terry: Who dreamt of Mom.

Adriana: I did.

Diana: Aww.

Terry. Can you tell me about that?

Adriana: I was actually talking about that today too.

Diana: Yeah.

Adriana: It wasn't of her being, like, gone. It was more so her alive. I don't fully remember the dream, but it was my birthday. My birthday was recent.

Terry: Oh. Happy birthday.

Adriana: Thank you. And it was the night of my birthday that I dreamt of it.

Terry: Oh so she visited you.

Diana: Aww.

Terry: Okay. Cool. You know why you didn't know she was passed?

Adriana: No.

Terry: She didn't want you to say goodbye again.

Diana: Aww.

Terry: Now when she comes again, and she will, she's going to appear even younger. Now can I ask how old Mom was when she passed?

Diana: Sixty-three.

Terry: Younger than me. Holy shit.

Diana: Yeah.

Terry: Young. So you're married, right?

Diana: Yes.

Terry: Where are the gay friends near you? She's putting gay.

Adriana: *Giggles*

Terry: Not you.

Diana: *Laughs* Whoa. Whoa.

Terry: No. No. Not you. Am I at work?

Diana: I don't know.

Terry: But she loves them.

Diana: Did she has gay friends as PS83?

Adriana: No. I don't think so.

Terry: And these are girls. Not guys.

Diana: Oh.

Terry: Two girls so I don't know what the proper terminology is.

Adriana: No.

Terry: Am I at work? Then maybe you don't know yet.

Diana: Yeah really.

Terry: She's saying, "It's not family". Oh you're going to be shocked when you find out who it is.

Adriana: Okay.

Diana: Wow.

Terry: Wow. Okay. Is Dad giving you a hard time about something?

Diana: Dad? Yes.

Adriana: Yes.

Terry: That's the frustration.

Adriana: Yes.

Terry: Okay. Is he being obstinate?

Diana: I mean, he's just, yeah.

Terry: Like stubborn. Obstinate.

Adriana: Stubborn. Frustrating.

Diana: Yeah.

Terry: Same thing. Obstinate. Stubborn.

Adriana: Uh huh.

Terry: He's angry.

Adriana: Uh huh.

Diana: Yes.

Terry: Very angry.

Diana: At the world.

Adriana: Yeah. Big time.

Terry: Yeah. Which one of you looks like Mom?

Adriana: Me.

Terry: Is he giving you a harder time?

Diana: Right now, yes.

Adriana: Sometimes

Terry. Okay. Listen, if there are emotions involved - like the opposite of love is apathy. You don't care one way or the other. Alright. Whatever. But frustration, anger, hatred; you're still emotionally attached. Who's Tommy?

Adriana: My boss.

Terry: She goes to work with you. So what do you do for a living?

Adriana: I'm an administrative assistant at an oil company.

Terry: At an oil company. Cool. She goes to work with you sometimes.

Diana: Aww.

Terry: She's let herself be known there though. So what are the coincidences? She's saying, I made myself known there.

Adriana: Is she opening my drawer?

Terry: Yeah. It's her.

Diana: Aww.

Adriana: That drawer does open all the time by itself. And actually, it hasn't done it in a while. My birthday was December tenth. When I walked in that morning that drawer was open.

Terry: Have you put your hand all the way in the back of the drawer? Did you forget that you had something in there? There's a reason she's opening the drawer. Okay. Who also has access to that desk?

Adriana: Anybody, really.

Terry: Okay. That's why she's opening the drawer. She wants you to take notice of what's in that drawer and then what's not in the drawer.

Diana: Wow.

Terry: Because she makes me feel things are getting moved around; switched around.

Adriana: Well, we have a cleaning company that cleans and everyday when we come in everything is moved over.

Terry: Not in the drawer. She's talking about inside the drawer.

Adriana: Inside the drawer?

Terry: That means somebody is actually purposely opening up your drawer and going in there.

Adriana: It's just like papers and stuff.

Terry: Keep it in mind. Is there a particular person at work you maybe don't trust completely?

Adriana: Not really.

Terry: Okay. Please keep it in mind. It's not random that she's opening the drawer. There's either something in there you forgot that's in there or someone's going in there and messing. She shows me twins. Now, don't get nervous girls. When I see twins either someone had twins, was a twin, two babies born twelve months apart. Doesn't have to be the same mother, but it has to be the same family. Is someone a twin? Did someone have twins?

Adriana: No

Diana: Not in our family. No.

Terry: Okay. She is talking about it. Does someone have a close friend that has two babies in the family? She is talking about twins. Oh my God this is going to be funny when you find out. Okay. You know to let your father talk because he's going to go from one opposite to the other opposite. "He doesn't even know what he's saying", your mother's saying.

Diana: Absolutely.

Terry: So why are you wasting your emotion on that? Can you believe Daddy's blah blah blah blah blah.

Diana: *Laughs* That is totally us.

Terry: Because that's what Mom is making me feel.

Adriana: Yes.

Terry: And then it almost seems like five minutes later it's something new and the complete opposite. And you want to go - that's why she makes me feel the frustration - but didn't you just say (the opposite). You know?

Diana: Yes. That's us.

Terry: Do you go head to head with him?

Adriana: Yeah.

Diana: At times.

Terry: Yeah. You don't though.

Diana: No.

Terry: So opposites. You guys are opposites.

Diana: Yes. I try to be the peacemaker.

Terry: You can't be. You're mother's saying, "don't". Why are you putting that kind of burden on you?

Diana: I know.

Terry: All you have to do for you to make yourself feel better is just be respectful. Now respect - see now she's going to this daughter. Respect doesn't mean you kiss his ass. But don't get in his face. You just say, listen, you know what? When maybe you're sane again and you want to call me I'm going to be here Dad. Do not go toe to toe with him because your mother is saying, "that's still your father".

Adriana: Right.

Terry: "Now you understand my frustration", she's saying. You think this is new? This isn't new.

Diana. No. It's not.

Terry: This is the way... Who was the drinker?

Diana: Him.

Terry: Oh. There you go.

Adriana: Yup.

Diana: Yes.

Terry: So that's why she says, "When you're sane again then you talk to me". You know you can't change a drinker. You can't. The love is for the drink.

Diana: Yes.

Terry: I want you to know something because Mom says you can tell them that part, an alcoholic will never take responsibility.

Diana: Absolutely.

Terry: You made me drink. See this. If you girls didn't do that I wouldn't have to drink. You don't live with him, do you?

Adriana: No.

Terry: Okay. Was he asking to live with you?

Diana: He wanted Adriana or George to live with him.

Terry: Oh really.

Adriana: He lives on his own.

Terry: "He has to live on his own", your mother is saying. You did the right thing.

Adriana: Yup.

Terry: He has to live on his own.

Diana: Yup.

Terry: You can't take care of an alcoholic. He's not a child. So how old is Dad?

Diana: Sixty-one.

Terry: Oh so he was a little younger than Mom.

Diana: Yes.

Terry: So he's still young.

Diana: He'll be sixty-two in a few weeks.

Terry: Yeah. He's still young. You know what? Your mother's saying what you have to do. So one of you - it might be you who's the enabler of him. You know, like you're understanding of it. You're enabling him. So the thing is if Dad wanted to live with your brother then let him go with the brother because he won't put up with it either. She doesn't want her girls to do that.

Adriana: Right.

Terry: Because I don't think the brother will enable him. He can drink himself, your brother.

Diana: Uh huh.

Terry: Because that's what Mom is saying. So he's not enabling him. They'll understand each other.

Adriana: Right.

Terry: Do you know what I mean?

Diana: Yes.

Terry: That's not your purpose in life. He's sixty-one. "Never let a parent reverse the roles", your mother is saying. "I never became a child to them. Their dad shouldn't be. He's not dependent on them. If they want to go off and drink, but I don't want that for my girls." Oh. She wrote seventy-six. What the hell?

Diana: I don't know.

Terry: Alright. Maybe, does July sixth mean something or - hold on. That's three. Forty-three. Is someone around the age of forty-three?

Diana: Oh. Yeah. My husband.

Terry: Okay. There you go. So she just wanted to cut in on her own self and just say hello to your husband.

Diana: She loves him. Nineteen seventy-six is...

Terry: But here's the thing. That's forty-three years ago. So if your husband is forty-three because she told me, "Can you do the subtraction?" Telepathically.

Diana: That's the year he was born.

Terry: Yeah. Okay. There you go. His words of advice to you about Dad; does he tell you, "Listen I think when it comes to your dad you should X"?

Diana: No. He would never say "to ex" my dad.

Terry: Not "ex" him. Like whatever he's going to say.

Adriana: Like she's not finishing it because it's whatever he tells you.

Terry: Yes. Right.

Diana: Like he doesn't condone him drinking and when he does, you know.

Terry: He's not telling you don't let him move in.

Diana: No. But I said, of course, God forbid my father didn't have a place to go we could put him in the basement and things like that. I would hate to see him, you know.

Terry: Your mother is saying no. Your family is your husband and your kids. Who's having stomach or digestive issues?

Adriana: That's like both of us.

Diana: Yeah. Constipation.

Terry: Alright, so I have like funny feelings in my stomach. You know if they mention it it's not going to be bad. Your father has a good heart. That's the problem. And he does love his daughters. And you're getting mixed up in it's tough love time for him.

Adriana: Yes.

Terry: Because he's been having weird thoughts lately. Like, I may start drinking a little more and your mother is saying, "Tell him to stop using me as an excuse".

Diana: Well, that's the problem.

Adriana: Mm hmm.

Diana: Yup

Terry: Because he's saying, "I'm so lonely. Your mother left me. I have no one. Blah blah blah."

Diana: Yup.

Terry: So your mother believes in drop dead dates meaning you have until this date and then I don't want to hear it anymore. So for him the drop dead date is the year anniversary of mom. That's not literally he's going to drop dead. They don't show me that. Now the year of firsts has ended.

Adriana: Yup. Almost.

Terry: Almost. Not yet. Now get on. Like, stop the drinking so much. She's not saying tell him now get on with your life. Go get a woman.

Diana: Right. No. No. Right.

Terry: That's not what she's saying. But she is saying stop using me as the excuse now for your current drinking situation.

Adriana: Right. Because she knows he's been drinking his whole life.

Terry: Yeah and that's not going to change. She says, "I understand it's a disease". Because her heart feels differently towards the son with the drinking because the mother would always try to help out a child. You can see where you can get into that enabling stuff, but she doesn't believe in that either. Do you know what she's trying to say? And it is a disease. It is. I'm telling you. So it's genetic. Hits more the boys than the girls. Although one of you is a dry drunk.

Diana: What is that?

Terry: There's a situation with the dry drunk. It's not a bad thing, but no one can tell you what to do. I'm doing it my way. Um. I like being alone sometimes.

Diana: Adriana.

Adriana: That's me.

Terry: There you go. Alright.

Adriana: That's me.

Terry: It's like that dry drowning which I never understood what that meant. You know what it means?

Adriana: Mm hmm.

Terry: Alright. So you don't even have to be in the water to drown.

Adriana: Right.

Terry: It's the same type of thing. So your personality will soften out later on in life. Not now. But it is helping you survive this.

Adriana: Mm hmm.

Terry: Were you dressed in funny hats or did Mom have a picture of herself in a funny hat?

Diana: She always dressed up for every holiday.

Terry: Funny hat. She's talking about a funny hat. This is not a dress hat. So this could be like a sombrero or a big hat.

Adriana: A Santa hat?

Terry: What kind of hat?

Adriana: A Santa hat?

Terry: No. That's not a funny hat. Is there a picture of her on the beach in this either beach hat or...

Diana: Maybe when she was younger.

Terry: She's talking about the picture with the funny hat in it.

Diana: I would have to look in the photo album.

Terry: Yeah. Look at the pictures. Okay. Also it is the number eleven. Not so much the clock. So keep that in mind.

Adriana: Really?

Terry: Yeah. She just showed me the eleven again. Okay. Who was supposed to go into the medical field? Did she ever want one of you to be a nurse or a doctor?

Adriana: A vet.

Terry: A vet. That's the medical field.

Adriana: Me.

Terry: And you didn't do it.

Adriana: No. I can't.

Diana: Aww.

Adriana: It's too sad for me. I can't be a vet. I would lose my mind.

Terry. Really?

Adriana: Yes. I wouldn't be able to handle it.

Terry: And who works with children?

Diana: I do.

Terry: You do. So she's just showing me. Are you a teacher?

Diana: Yes.

Terry: Oh cool. In the Bronx?

Diana: Yes.

Terry: The big tree. She calls it a special tree. Do you guys own your property? Do you have a multifamily house?

Adriana: No.

Terry: Where's the multifamily? She visits someone in a multifamily house. Or it could be a single house with more than one family living in it.

Adriana: What's considered a multifamily house?

Terry: A two family is multifamily. Or you could have a house that has three levels and three different families living in it.

Adriana: No. I'm in a building now that has all different...

Terry: That's a multifamily house.

Adriana: And there's a tree there.

Diana: A co-op.

Adriana: And it's decorated for Christmas. I just looked at it the other day too. Right when you pull into the parking lot.

Terry: She was with you.

Diana: Aw.

Terry: It's near the multifamily house. Apartment building is multifamily. And did you have your closing? Did you put the money down on this already?

Adriana: Mm hmm.

Terry: When did you have your closing?

Adriana: November eighteenth.

Terry: November.

Diana: Aw.

Terry: That's how she does it. So she knows. That's why she mentioned November: one, one, one, eight.

Adriana: Yup. Yup. And I move in November twenty-ninth. So yeah. November.

Terry: I can not believe you didn't remember that. Who gets anemic or low blood or...

Diana: Me.

Terry: You do. You have it now.

Diana: I just went to the doctor and the doctor checked my blood.

Terry: Your mother doesn't care. Now, if they mention it it'll be fine. She doesn't believe in these doctors.

Diana: Oh jeez.

Adriana: We don't either.

Terry: They missed it. It's not like dangerously low or anything like that, but it is off right now.

Adriana: Your white blood cells are low though.

Terry: Oh. There you go. The blood. Oh there you go.

Adriana: And she's going next week to retest it.

Terry: Okay good because you're off - blood wise. Okay so Mom knows that. Good news is she mentioned it. So if she mentions it it'll be okay. Who is Paul, Paula, Pauline, Paulo? Why is she mentioning this name?

Adriana: ███████ is our uncle and then there's also ███████ who was her friend.

Terry: Okay. What's going on with ███████?

Diana: He's disabled. He lives with her sister.

Terry: Oh so it's her brother-in-law?

Adriana: Yes.

Terry: Was this the sister she mentioned before?

Adriana: Yes.

Terry: Okay. So again, she went there to check out that situation. That's why she mentions ███████. Is it something with his legs?

Adriana: Mm hmm.

Terry: Okay.

Diana: It's one of the many things.

Terry: Oh. There's a lot?

Adriana: Mm hmm.

Terry: How old is he?

Diana: Late sixties.

Terry: Who made pastina? Did someone recently make it?

Diana: Not recently.

Terry: Okay. Because she's showing me pastina. Remember this could be current or a memory. Is there a place you guys go called Pastinas?

Diana: Patsy's.

Terry: What's this?

Adriana: There's a Pastina's, but we've never been there. On Central Avenue.

Terry: Is there? "You should go", she's saying. You'll have a great time.

Adriana: Kristen's been telling me to go too.

Terry: Oh. When did Kristen tell you to go there?

Adriana: A couple of weeks ago.

Terry: There you go. That's what she's saying.

Adriana: She used to eat pastina too.

Terry: Did she? There you go. So go.

Adriana: We're going to Pastina's. Maybe we'll have a Christmas dinner there.

Terry: You're not doing anything on Christmas day? You're not celebrating, huh?

Adriana: I don't really want to.

Terry: But you have children though, right?

Diana: I've been cooking, but the holidays have been horrible.

Terry: I can't even imagine. Well, I can't say that. We lost my nephew in March so, you know. I can imagine. I remember when my dad passed. He lived with me so I was very close to him because my mother and father were divorced. It's difficult.

Adriana: I remember that from the book.

Terry: Oh you read my book!

Adriana: Yes. I didn't finish it because I don't want to finish it.

Diana: We read most of it.

Adriana: Like, I don't want the book to end.

Terry: We're making another one.

Adriana: Good. Great. Because I don't want the book to end.

Terry: I'll do another one. Do you want your mother to be in my next book?

Adriana: Yes!

Terry: Seriously? You have to write a little biography about her and you have to remember when you came to me because I can't pull it up by the name, and I'll put her in my book. You know what the book is called? The Story Of Eight. I'm choosing eight people.

Adriana: That's where the eight is from.

Terry: I'm taking a shower. Someone tells me, "You have to write the book. The title is The Story Of Eight". I look it up and it's a very spiritual number which I didn't know. Is there something wrong with one of the windows where you live?

Adriana: The screen is out.

Terry: Okay. She wants that done.

Adriana: So do I.

Terry: So make sure. But you had your closing already.

Adriana: Yes.

Terry: And it wasn't on the punch list.

Adriana: No. There's a couple things in this place that weren't involved.

Terry: Yeah, but now tough luck.

Adriana: Yeah.

Terry: Oh. Okay. By the way, with the children - how old are your children?

Diana: Noelle is going to be fifteen and Sean just turned eleven.

Terry: Okay. So your mother's telling me what the eleven means.

Diana: Her grandson.

Terry: Who's Teddy? Ted, Teddy.

Diana: A friend of the family. One of my father's close friends.

Terry: Okay. Living though. This one is not passed. She's saying, "Living".

Diana: Yes.

Terry: Okay. Does your father have a temper like I could punch the wall?

Adriana: Yes.

Diana: Yes.

Terry: Because your mother is showing me that. You know if your brother and him live together there's going to be fights; physical fights.

Diana: Yeah. That's why they can never live together.

Adriana: Yeah. We know that.

Terry: And he can't live with either one of you.

Diana: No.

Adriana: No.

Terry: Not you. "You'll be thrown out", she's saying, of where you are. Not you because she doesn't want her grandchildren exposed to it.

Adriana: So my co-op right now is both of ours. Like, he cosigned for me.

Terry: So he just cosigned. He doesn't own it.

Adriana: Yeah. So technically, owning wise it's me and him, but he does not live there. And he will not live there.

Terry: No. He can't live there. Which one of you can sing? Well, whether they can sing or not, who sings in the house? Or in the car?

Adriana: Oh. I sing all the time in the car.

Terry: Oh. There you go.

Adriana: Is she with me when I'm singing?

Terry: Yeah. Are you bilingual?

Diana: No.

Terry: Why is she trying to speak to me in another language? Was she bilingual?

Diana: I mean, we're Italian.

Terry: Yeah. So am I, but I don't speak it.

Diana: No. She never spoke it around us.

Terry. Alright so who's the friend around you that's bilingual? That could be Spanish also. Remember, it doesn't have to be Italian. Am I at work? Am I a neighbor? I think I'm going to you and I think I'm going to be living in that apartment building.

Adriana: In my building?

Terry: Yeah. Your new building.

Adriana: Maybe the lady across from me, Margarita. Maybe she speaks Italian. Didn't she ask me if I spoke Italian when she found out we were Italian? I'm almost positive she did.

Diana: I don't remember. I could see her speaking Italian.

Terry: Okay. So Margarita speaks Italian? Or you have to find out because she likes this woman who's bilingual; living.

Adriana: Really? Because she seems a little cookey to me.

Terry: Well, she's no Tina she says.

Adriana: The first day I moved in she had her cat like literally just walk into my house and like roam my whole house.

Terry: Really? She just wanted to make sure there were no mice in there. Because cats will smell them.

Adriana: Well I have a cat, but he wasn't there yet.

Terry: Oh. Okay. I think she was actually trying to do you a favor by letting the cat just walk in.

Adriana: Right.

Diana: She seems nice.

Adriana: Yeah. I really feel like she asked, "Do you guys speak Italian?" And we were like, "Oh no we don't".

Terry: Alright. Because Mom was there. "There's no hiding the spare key again," she says. So, where you live now, who hides the spare key? Because she makes me feel it's under something and there's no hiding a spare key, she saying. Oh my God this is going to be important. Okay so listen. You may need someone to service something and you're not going to be there and they say to leave the spare key... and your mother's saying no.

Adriana: I was supposed to give a spare key to my Super.

Terry: There you go.

Adriana: On my rules it says give a set of keys to the Super for emergencies. So she's telling me not to do that.

Terry: No. You have to. That's part of the rules. They can start giving you a problem with that.

Diana: You just have to be careful.

Terry: Yeah. You just have to be careful.

Adriana: I haven't done it yet. It hasn't been brought up to me or anything.

Terry: Perfect.

Diana: Then don't say anything.

Terry: Don't say anything. Is your eleven year old a boy?

Diana: Yes.

Terry: Is he artistic? Not autistic. Artistic. Or is he very sensitive?

Diana: He's sensitive.

Terry: Okay. Because that to me will come in as if you're creative you have a different type of energy. And is the other one a girl?

Diana: Yes.

Terry: Okay. She's nothing like him.

Diana: No.

Terry: She's the complete opposite.

Diana: Complete opposite.

Terry: Like this. *Points to both sisters*

Adriana: Yes.

Terry: That's what your mother's saying. Just like this.

Diana: Yes.

Terry: She has them. Okay. You're your son and you're her daughter.

Diana: Yes.

Terry: That's what your mother is saying.

Adriana: That is great.

Terry: What?

Diana: Adriana's her godmother.

Terry: I was just going there. Okay. Who's Vin?

Adriana: We know a ████████. Close family friend.

Terry: Does he work with his hands?

Diana: He's an architect.

Terry: He is. Okay so he does. I don't know. He may be part of your future when it comes to…

Adriana: *Laughs*

Terry: No. No. Let me finish.

Diana: Oh boy.

Terry: If there's a problem in the co-op he may be part of your future.

Diana: Oh. To fix things.

Terry: Yeah. Or let's say there's a constant problem. If he's an architect he can be looking and say the reason is because of this line. That's what she means. She's not saying anything. "You're not ready for that step anyway", she's saying.

Adriana: I agree.

Terry: At all.

Adriana: I agree.

Terry: And leave her alone about it, your mother's saying. You're a baby though. You both are. How young are you?

Adriana: Thirty-one.

Terry: Yeah. You're a baby. Oh my God. I have a granddaughter who's twenty. She does mention ███████. Who's ███████?

Diana: That's my uncle's sister-in-law.

Terry: And what's going on?

Diana: Deceased.

Terry: Okay. Fine. Because she mentions ███████. Okay. Because I hear the name. She says, "Could you mention ███████"? So if I only hear the name I don't know what side of the table I'm going to.

Adriana: Right.

Diana: Okay.

Terry: But she does hang out with her and she's
fine. Okay? And she mentions Rena. Who's Rena?
R. E. N. A.

Diana: Living?

Terry: This one is living.

Adriana: She had a friend Rena when she worked
at school.

Terry: Okay.

Adriana: And there's another lady, Rena, who was
one of my friend's mothers.

Terry: This one is living.

Adriana: Yeah.

Diana: They're both living.

Adriana: Yeah. She was a crossing guard. They
used to see each other a lot and talk to her.

Terry: Okay. Who is the heavier one?

Adriana: The one she worked with I want to say.

Terry: That's the one she's talking about.

Adriana: She was very sickly.

Terry: Okay. That's what she's talking about. And she's living. Both of them are living, but she wants to go to the heavier one. Because she does visit her.

Adriana: I don't definitely know if she's heavier.

Terry: Okay. So you'll figure it out. Now she could be speaking about when they were in their prime because they show me them, usually, in their prime.

Adriana: She used to be good friends with her when they worked together and then when our mom got sick Rena reached out to her because she had many different types of cancer and she was sick, but she's alive still.

Terry: She's doing this, your mom. *touches right breast* Did she have any breast issues?

Diana: I mean…

Adriana: Are you talking about Mom or Rena?

Terry: Not Rena.

Diana: Mom had tumors.

Terry: In the breast?

Diana: No it was more in the lungs, but they were protruding.

Adriana: Here and here.

Terry: Oh. So they were coming out. So that's why. You have the tree?

Diana: *Laughs*

Terry: Why is she telling me that?

Diana: I put up my Christmas tree on Saturday.

Terry: You did.

Diana: And I didn't want to put it up.

Terry: But you did. "Thank you", she's saying. Thank you.

Diana: I put it up for her.

Adriana: She put it up Saturday, but all day Saturday she kept saying, "Mom, give me a sign. Mom, give me a sign" and her T.V. started turning on and off. So she put the tree up.

Terry: So now she's telling you. She's saying, "Now I have the voice", meaning me, tonight. She's very proud. It was not easy. At all.

Diana: No. It wasn't.

Terry: No. But it's because of God that she's here. She says, "I'm not getting religious or anything like that, but the fact of the matter is I am talking to them. So I'm better". She says, "I see you guys everyday". Who's Dylan? Who knew Dylan? Or knows Dylan? Is there a Dylan near one of your children in the classroom?

Diana: No.

Terry: Okay. I'm going to write that name. She likes this kid. It's either a kid... I think it's a kid. Dylan. She likes this one. Put presents under the tree for her and for you guys, she's saying.

Diana: There's no Christmas without you Mom.

Terry: That's why she's there. She's saying, "That's why I'm here".

Diana: She loved Christmas more than anyone we know.

Terry: Where's the skirt for the tree? She's missing a skirt.

Diana: Maybe a tree skirt. I have my tree skirt. But maybe she's talking about her tree.

Adriana: Her tree is missing the star. The tree at my father's house is missing the star. I don't know if the skirt is on. I don't think it is, actually.

Diana: I don't know. We haven't seen it.

Adriana: I saw it on Friday, but there was no star. I don't remember if there was a skirt.

Terry: She has to be honest with you girls. She doesn't go there.

Adriana: Yeah?

Terry: Not near that tree. The energy there is a little heavy in that house so she can't. She can't. Even though you're in mourning, the energy is not that heavy. I mean, it's heavy, but it's not where she can't get because of your children. They bring her in. Do you find your son just randomly touching you or patting you? Or rubbing like this.

Diana: He consoled me Saturday night.

Terry: That's what she's showing me.

Diana: I was trying to decorate the tree and I opened a bag and I was crying and he came and hugged me. So she was there?

Terry: She was there. She's just relaying what she saw. And when is the year?

Diana: January fifth.

Terry: Oh right before little Christmas. She was home on little Christmas, she's saying. She's calling that home.

Adriana: Her husband's birthday is January seventh.

Terry: When is it?

Diana: January seventh.

Terry: Oh no. Oh my God. I'm just getting the full impact of that. So she was being waked on his birthday?

Adriana: No. On the eighth. And her funeral was on Sophia's birthday, which is her daughter's.

Diana: My daughter.

Adriana: The eighth.

Terry: The number eight. The baking. Were you going to make it or did Mom used to make this certain thing Christmas time?

Diana: She baked every year an Easter cake; a bunny cake that Adriana and I baked last year for her.

Terry: No. She's talking about Christmas.

Diana: She wanted to bake cookies with Sophia and she didn't get to last year.

Terry: Okay. Do that for her. You can help her.

Diana: She actually has a baking kit that her sister bought her.

Adriana: That's weird because I just recently got baking stuff too.

Terry: So all of you just be together. Have the music playing. You don't have to listen to Christmas songs, but have music playing because what it does for her daughter's is it raises their energy.

Diana: Yup.

Terry: She sees you every single day, this woman. Every single day.

Diana: We feel her all the time.

Terry: Because you have to know she's there. And she's also doing… did someone say to you you shouldn't talk to them or they won't rest in peace?

Diana: People say that we shouldn't come here to talk to her sometimes because they have to rest.

Terry: They don't rest on the other side because they don't have a body. That's what she's saying.

Diana: She's everywhere.

Terry: Yeah. "She has to be everywhere", she saying.

Adriana: Oh Daddy too.

Diana: Oh Daddy. Perfect.

Adriana: He is one hundred percent against this. He wants to go to Saint Raymond's every day of his life. I think I told you this last time. He wants to go to Saint Ramond's everyday of his life to see his wife and we finally told him she's not there.

Terry: She's not.

Adriana: A couple of months ago he actually told us, "I think it's disgusting you forgot about your mother. You don't go to Saint Raymond's". And I was like, that's bullshit.

Terry: Here's the thing though, but you were half right. She's not there, but the obligation on that side is if someone's going to the cemetery to talk to them they have to go. They don't go and lay down so they're standing right by your side listening to what you have to say. You leave. They leave. Sometimes they'll get in the car with you and follow you home. Sometimes they just go visiting. And that's their obligation on the other side. But to live there, they don't.

Diana: Right.

Terry: They don't. And you have a memorial for her in your house.

Diana: Yeah. We do.

Terry: That's what she's telling me so what's he talking about? Who's Frank? She said, "Frank's here". And I'm passed.

Adriana: Oh. Passed?

Terry: So Frank can be Frank, Franny, Francis. And I'm equal to Mom and Dad. That's your big "Aha" moment.

Adriana: I don't know a Frank that passed away.

Diana: Neither do I.

Terry: Yeah. This one is passed. Dark hair. Light eyes and I knew Rich. Alright so let's work backwards a little bit.

Adriana: I knew Rich, but who's Frank?

Terry: Well he did give me his name. Rich has to be living. Is Rich living?

Diana: The Rich we know is not.

Terry: No. This one is living. Rich, Rick, Ricky, Richard. Alright. Don't worry about it. You'll figure that out. Okay. So you know about the paper and you know about the three informal prayers.

Adriana: Yes.

Terry: Your mother said if your father gives you a hard time about this just tell him it's in his bible.

Diana: Which he's not religious at all either.

Terry: She's not. But…

Diana: He's not, I'm saying. He's the least religious person we know.

Terry: Okay. Listen, your mother is telling me to tell you that if he tries to prove a point he's going to become religious for the moment and to counteract it, it's the doubting Thomas story. Thomas didn't believe Christ was walking the earth.

Diana: Like he doesn't believe.

Adriana: He doesn't believe, but when we told him last time about it he was like, "I don't believe. I don't believe". But then I found out he was telling a bunch of people about it. So then my whole thing was if you don't believe why are you going and telling people about it.

Terry: Alright. So those three prayers, informal, by the heart, people living: Someone you care about, don't know, don't like. The person you don't like, or trust, the prayer goes something like, Dear God, please.... Rosie's there, also. She's interrupting me. Let me just finish this. Dear God, please let them find their way, but keep them away from me. Rosie was a little older than her. Rose, Rosey, Rosa, Rosemary, Rosemarie.

Diana: Living?

Terry: No. This one is passed. Little older than her. Could have been an old neighbor because I don't feel I'm family because she doesn't show me the blood sign.

Adriana: I don't know.

Terry: Okay. Keep that in mind.

A Letter from Diana and Adriana

☆ ★ ☆ ★ ☆ ★ ☆ ★

Angela was a devoted daughter to her mother. She was Mommy's little girl, always by her mother's side. Growing up was hard for her and her sister. Their father was not in the picture, so their mother played both roles; mother and father. That is why it was extremely hard when her mom got sick and passed away when Angela was still so young.

Losing her mom at a young age made her the strong and independent woman that she was. She looked up to her older sister for guidance and support. Angela had to teach herself how to survive in the real world. She got a job at a young age and was always a hard worker. Angela's dream was to get married and have a family of her own one day. At twenty-three, she fell in love with a man who was dressed in all white. At first, she thought he worked for good humor. After beating him in a game of shuffleboard, the rest is history. About forty years of marriage and three kids later, Angela absolutely adored her family. There was nothing that made her happier than being with her family.

Angela was Christmas. She loved everything about Christmas, from decorating to Christmas shopping. She would spend many days and nights at the mall shopping. When we were kids, our mom used to sit at the dining room table singing Christmas songs while wrapping presents all night. Christmas morning was always so much fun as a child. We would wake up early, but not too early because mom liked to sleep late, mostly because she was up all hours of the night wrapping the gifts and making sure everything was perfect for Christmas morning. Mom would get so excited when we would open our gifts and would save the big gifts from "Santa" for last. Mom always made sure we got all the presents on our Christmas lists.

Angela loved spending time with her daughters. She would refer to our time together as "Girls Day." We would go out for lunch, which most of the time was Apple Bee's, which was Angela's absolute favorite. She always ordered the same thing every time - honey barbeque boneless wings and oriental chicken salad. And we can not forget about dessert. Ice cream was Angela's favorite. We used to tease her and tell her she loved ice cream more than food. After enjoying a delicious lunch, we would go next door to the movies. Angela would always have to make time to get her snacks - Goobers were a must. After that, we would sit through the whole movie laughing and sometimes even crying. These memories will always stay in our hearts forever.

SIX

☆ ★ ☆ ★ ☆ ★ ☆ ★

Helen is one of three women that came to see me for a group reading. For the sake of the book, I only transcribed Helen's story. Upon the arrival of the three women, I had a strong sense of a young man with dark, long hair entering behind one of these women. When I say our loved ones are never far away I really mean it. This young man was an important part of the reading. Not only did he have messages to give, he did it with a sense of humor that had the entire room laughing. Laughing is healing. Healing is important. Never be embarrassed to laugh through your pain. It just means you're on your road to recovery.

☆ ★ ☆ ★ ☆ ★ ☆ ★

∞ The Story of Eight ∞

Helen's Reading

☆ ★ ☆ ★ ☆ ★ ☆ ★

Terry: I'm going to leave this digital recorder on, so it will pick everything up. Sometimes, it's rare, but it has happened, it'll pick up static and that's *them*. Are you ready? Because I need your attention before we start. The month of August. What does any day in August, or the eighth of any month, or the number eight mean to you?

Helen: We lost my son.

Terry: How old is your son?

Helen: Twenty-four.

Terry: Okay. Did he have dark hair?

Helen: Yes. And long.

Terry: Long dark hair.

Helen: Yeah.

Terry: He's saying, "You took your blessed time in coming".

Helen: *Laughs* I can see that.

Terry: He's in a very jovial, happy mood.

Helen: Good.

Terry: And he's apologizing. "I'm sorry," he's saying. "I'm sorry. I'm sorry for it all". He just gave me a newspaper. I have to figure out why. It doesn't have to be him. He could be trying to tell me about someone else. Was someone written up in a newspaper?

Helen: He was.

Terry: He was. So what was that about?

Helen: His death.

Terry: His passing. How did he pass? Did he hit his head?

Helen: Yes.

Terry: Alright, so he's here. He wants to say hello to you.

Helen: Hey Brian.

Terry: "Mom, I need more singing and music."

Helen: Oh yeah. That was our thing. *Laughs*
That's definitely Brian.

Terry: How long ago did he pass?

Helen: It's going to be five years this August. He
died in an elevator shaft and his head was crushed.

Terry: Oh my God. He made the news. That's what
he's saying, "I made the news. It's a bad way to
make it".

Helen: *Laughs* He's such a jerk.

Terry: "But that's who I am," he's saying. "You know
this"

Helen: Yes, he is. *Laughs*

Terry: He's with a gentleman…

Helen: Yes.

Terry: Well, let me finish. You may think you know
and you may not. Alright? Because he's bringing
out a flag and I have to figure out why. He's
showing me the American flag. Was someone in
the military? He's playing a trick. I'll let him do it.
Was someone associated with the patriotic months
that we have, which would be July or November or

September? July is the Fourth of July. September, unfortunately, was 9/11 or November, which is Veteran's Day. Does that make sense to you? Or did someone always have the flag? Did they wear something with the flag on it? He's showing me the flag. Okay. That might be an "Aha" moment. I don't want you to try to fit it in. You may say to yourself, "Oh, that's what it was".

Helen: Okay.

Aha Moment: After the reading, Helen sent a message to explain:

"The person that was in the Military at the time, was my daughter, his sister Elyce. They were very close siblings. She was so upset."

Terry: The last month - the month that I got. Not what he was doing - was March. So any day in March, the third of any month, the number three, the names Joseph, Joe, Joanne because for me this is Saint Joseph's month.

Helen: March.

Terry: And what's March?

Helen: That's George.

Terry: And who's George?

Helen: My father.

Terry: Is he on the other side?

Helen: Yeah.

Terry: Okay. There you go. Did he have a lot of hair?

Helen: Yes.

Terry: Okay. He's always with you, this gentleman. Always.

Helen: Yeah. He died the day after my birthday.

Terry: Wow. He passed, he's saying. "I passed over. I just went from one life to another." Now, I'm looking at you, but I'm looking through you because I'm trying to keep up with what they're trying to show me. Did you sue?

Helen: Yes.

Terry: Did you win?

Helen: We're still ongoing.

Terry: You will. "Stop with the memorial", he's saying. So do you have his ashes or a special place in your house to mourn?

Helen: Yes.

Terry: Alright, so I know what he means. Listen, it's easy for them to say. They're not connected to their body any longer.

Helen: I know.

Terry: It's a room of sadness. So this makes perfect sense to me. You ready? I saw this sign one other time, and I thought it meant something literally. I saw a polar bear and when I mentioned a polar bear, this woman said, "Oh my God! That was my son's favorite." She lost her son also. The polar bear. The spiritual meaning, and this is going to be for the whole family, is you need to surrender and accept. "And I'm in the light of God." Now, I saw the Holy Spirit while I was praying. He comes in as a dove. This is not a religious reading, but I am a spiritual medium. That means from the light of God. So he's in the good place. Also, he's the one who sent Archangel Michael. Now let me talk to you about Archangel Michael. He's the protector. Archangel Michael is also the patron saint of police officers and firefighters. So either someone has a connection or affiliation with a police officer or firefighter, someone has some part of this gift and they need to know how to protect against not letting in all the energies. Your son is looking at you. And his month, Archangel Michael's month, is September. Your son is the one that brought in

Archangel Michael - for a few reasons, he's telling me. Oh, so either the name Michael or Michelle can mean something, because the feminine version of Michael is Michelle. Is there a person in the family who has not found themselves yet? Meaning career wise. I don't know what I'm going to do. Because he's suggesting police officer or firefighter because they need to feel like part of a positive group and there is comradery with police officers or firefighters. Even volunteer firefighters. Something of that nature. I hate to ask you this, but I have to. I know he didn't have any hand in his passing and it happened so quick, so quick. This is a good thing what I'm showing you. I'm telling you, I saw this guy coming in. He's holding a flag. So I passed years ago. Years ago. And your son was like, "What?" And the guy said, "Don't look". But your son looked. He said, "Who's that?" And the gentleman said, "That was you". Then the curse words started. "Are you f-ing kidding me? Oh my God! Oh my God!" He didn't feel it. He felt the fear. Like, "What? I'm confused". He was already out of body before, which is also what happened to a firefighter from 9/11 - I read his family. When he came in, he told them what they felt in 9/11 was fear and heat. When they jumped, they were already out of their bodies. They never felt that because Archangel Michael had his wings out. Every one of them came to him like a magnet. And Archangel Michael is watching over your son in particular. Okay? Alright. Who's suffering from stomach issues? So it could be digestive problems. Digestive could be my stomach's been off, my intestines, my bowels, anything with digestion. Yes. He's telling me,"Yes."

Helen: Yeah. Not me.

Terry: It doesn't have to be. It can be any energy that touches you.

Helen: It could be Amber.

Terry: Okay. Who's Amber?

Helen: Amber is my daughter.

Terry: Okay. So he just wants to say hello to your daughter. It's more nerves. Now all the sudden your son thinks he's a doctor on the other side.

Helen: He's always been.

Terry: Okay. He's full of himself. In a nice way.

Helen: *Laughs*

Terry: Sorry. That's not in a bad way.

Helen: No. We're good. It's true. That's him. That's his personality.

Terry: By the way, there is a baby. Your son is holding a baby. Did you lose a baby?

Helen: Did I lose a baby?

Terry: It could be either miscarriage or this baby wasn't born. Does that make sense to you?

Helen: Yes.

Terry: Okay. There you go.

Helen: And Elyce, my daughter, had two miscarriages.

Terry: Okay. I know I'm a boy, but it's not your daughter because he's saying, "I have a brother with me." Okay? So he's holding a brother. So he says, "Tell my mother we're not statues like all I do all day is just sit here like the Virgin Mary holding a baby. That's not what I'm doing".

Helen: *Laughs*

Terry: "I'm just bringing the baby in to say hello. That's all I'm doing. Because you have to explain things to my mother."

Helen: Oh wow.

Terry: Sorry, but I'm only going by him. I don't know him, so I should pre-apologize.

Helen: *Laughs* We're good.

Terry: Okay. Now there is a lady, but it's the scent of her perfume and she makes me feel like she was known by this certain scent. It's a beautiful scent, but it was light. It wasn't heavy. So I haven't read the pencil yet, just so you know. These loved ones are really strong on the other side. They're just speaking to me. The pencil actually isn't for my benefit. It's for yours because it makes you concentrate and that tells them to start lining up. It was the scent. "My perfume." You're going to start smelling it again in the house. Now, I don't think I'm this grandmother I'm speaking to.

Helen: No.

Terry: No. This is someone else. Another female. Does that make sense to you? I'm looking at you, but I'm not waiting for an answer. I'm speaking to her. Okay. I'm associated with the woman whose nails were always done. They had to be done. I would not go out unless I look good, but especially my nails had to be done. Does that make any sense to you?

Helen: *Nods*

Terry: Do you know Lauren, Laurel, Lori? Something like that.

Helen: Laura.

Terry: Who's Laura?

Helen: My cousin's daughter.

Terry: How old?

Helen: I'm not sure. She's like twenty-five.

Terry: Alright. There's going to be good news coming around her.

Helen: This is true. She's getting married.

Terry: Oh. When is she getting married?

Helen: September first.

Terry: There you go.

Helen: And there's September.

Terry: There's your September. Okay. So they're going to be there.

Helen: Oh. So nice.

Terry: Your son's not going.

Helen: *Laughs*

Terry: He's saying, "I'm not going to go to this."

Helen: Why not?

Terry: Sorry. "Nothing bad. I just have other things to do."

Helen: *Laughs* I can see that he has.

Terry: "That's not my thing right now."

Helen: No.

Terry: He is putting singing near you. Do you sing in the house?

Helen: *Nods*

Terry: Oh, you do. "Very nice," he's saying. "But that move that you do when you're singing…"

Helen: *Laughs*

Terry: So, do you try to dance when you sing or is there a particular move?

Helen: I guess so.

Terry: Okay. He's saying, "But that move". Okay. Can we go? Oh, the neck. My neck is hurting me. This is not your son because logically if you damaged your head your neck is just as damaged.

Helen: Right.

Terry: He's talking about someone living. Has someone been complaining that their neck is stiff or they think they're sleeping wrong? The pain he's giving me - he's touching me from here down to my shoulder.

Helen: I mean, someone had an accident. We almost lost her.

Terry: Okay. There you go. But you didn't from the grace of Archangel Michael.

Helen: Yeah. It was incredible.

Terry: Yeah. This person should have passed, but it was because of Archangel Michael. Now was this after your son's passing?

Helen: It was just recently. Memorial Day weekend. She's still walking around with a neck brace.

Terry: Okay. Guess what? He's saying, "You're welcome". Then Archangel Michael looks at him like, are you kidding? You know. She needs to say her prayers because she almost went there.

Helen: I believe it. It was incredible the way that happened.

Terry: Yeah. It doesn't make any sense that she's walking.

Helen: It doesn't.

Terry: That's what he's telling me.

Helen: Yeah.

Terry: Okay. Let's start reading the pencil. The family divide. What is he speaking of? You know what it is?

Helen: Yes.

Terry: Okay. You don't have to acknowledge it because he just put a black curtain down. That means it's not my business. It doesn't mean he's making a judgment on it. It doesn't mean it's evil, or it's going to get worse. It just means, in a nice way, you don't need confirmation. Which is fine. Okay. "Because people always have an opinion," he's saying. Not him, but people talk in the ear. Talk in the ear. And then you get the smile. But go with your gut feeling. There is an origination point, he's saying. Okay. Oh, he just brought in a nice-looking dog. With this dog, I would consider the dog a protector dog. This is not a chihuahua, although chihuahua would think they were German Shepherds. So I could be a Rottie, a Pit...

Helen: An American Bulldog?

Terry: Okay. Yeah. They are definitely protectors. So was this your dog?

Helen: Yes.

Terry: Okay. It shits all over the place.

Helen: *Laughs*

Terry: They keep him outside.

Helen: *Laughs* He's not happy about that. He wants to be inside.

Terry: Okay. So just so you know. Because anything that grows has a soul. Anything with a soul goes to the other side. Okay? He wants to give you a lion. So either that's a favorite thing of yours or a Leo because Leo is a lion. I'm an August child. That's why my protector is a lion. He can come in with a pit, but I have a lion on the other side. He wants to give it to you. What's with the baby pictures?

Helen: I don't have baby pictures.

Terry: He's talking about baby pictures.

Helen: I brought pictures though.

Terry: Can I see them? I can look at them if you don't mind, but the baby pictures. It's all baby pictures all over the place. What's he speaking of?

Helen: I don't know.

Terry: He goes to a place and sees baby pictures. *Looks at pictures* So your son is in here, right?

Helen: Yes.

Terry: Baby pictures. Are you kidding me? These are baby pictures. It doesn't have to be an infant. When they were babies. Your babies.

Helen: But we all have pictures on the walls of our children, yeah?

Terry: No. He's talking about baby pictures. *Flips through pictures* So he's telling me something and I want to see if you see this. Look here. That's a gentleman's face that was on the other side already when this picture was taken.

Helen: That's scary.

Terry: No. How do you know it's not family? This gentleman had a long face. Did he ever ride a motorcycle?

Helen: Not that I know of.

Terry: Okay. Remember the friend?

Helen: That rode the motorcycle? That was down the block. He died.

Terry: Okay. That's what he's talking about.

Helen: Oh wow. That was Chris. He died of a motorcycle accident.

Terry: Did he have nightmares or bad dreams when he was living?

Helen: Yeah.

Terry: He was gifted.

Helen: Oh yeah. We all knew that.

Terry: On some level, he knew he wasn't going to be on this earth for too long. He didn't fit in. He was gifted and gifted is not cursed. It's gifted.

Helen: I know.

Terry: And that's why I saw the Holy Spirit. And no wonder why he's hanging with this Archangel like they're friends. But it makes sense to me because I will tell you any blessing - crosses, blessings and gifts - are all the same. One thing is all three. He had his share. You know what I mean? What sister - you have daughters right?

Helen: Yeah.

Terry: What daughter was most like him?

Helen: Elyce.

Terry: She's going to start having the same gift he did. Which one is Elyce in this one? *Shows picture* This is her? Okay. So she's going to be prompted in the arts somehow. Either writing or...

Helen: She's extremely talented. Yeah.

Terry: Yeah. Because she's being led by them on the other side. It could get to a point though where I can go to sleep and let's say I want to write something. Maybe I like putting words on paper. And I wake up and it's like, "Oh my God I have to write that down". So she's going to have to learn - where your son didn't know how to set boundaries - she's going to have to learn them and he's trying to get to her. Now, he's going to someone's throat. Did someone have thyroid issues or was their throat their trauma area? Maybe I always get sore throats or bronchitis. What's with the throat? Or it could be acid reflux. It's going through the throat. It's for someone living. Not for someone passed.

Helen: Maybe C.J. because he has sleep apnea issues.

Terry: Oh. There you go because you go *snort snort snort*.

Helen: Yeah.

Terry: And your heart will stop *snort*.

Helen: Yeah.

Terry: So this is his brother?

Helen: Yes.

Terry: So he watches over him as well. Who's having a problem with keys or locks?

Helen: *Laughs* Me.

Terry: What's going on?

Helen: I don't know what happened the other day. I tried to open my door.

Terry: And it didn't work.

Helen: It didn't open, and I tried to push it in and it didn't open.

Terry: He just keeps saying, "Oh sorry".

Helen: *Laughs*

Terry: He was there with you. That's a pretty current event.

Helen: And then I closed it and I opened it again and it just flung open.

Terry: Yeah. He knows that. That's a sign. "But I had to get your attention," he's saying. Is there a picture of someone on the beach where they think their shit doesn't stink and they're taking a picture like this? *Strikes a pose*

Helen: That's Elyce.

Terry: Who's this?

Helen: My daughter just did that picture.

Terry: How long ago?

Helen: That was this May. Just recently.

Terry: He's making fun of it.

Helen: He should. *Laughs* She looked gorgeous.

Terry: Yeah. Like your shit doesn't stink. Now, what he's going to start doing is appearing in pictures. Just like this one appeared. You won't see it, but he's going to come in as an orb. An orb is perfectly round or they can make it overdeveloped, meaning, let's say this is me in a picture *draws*. This is why I failed art. Let's say you're taking it with your phone camera. The picture before that is fine. This picture will have a big white spot like it's overdeveloped and then the picture after that is fine. That's the picture he's in. So it's going to start to happen.

Helen: That's good.

Terry: Okay.

Helen: Okay. Nothing has changed.

Terry: He's better looking if that's possible, he's saying.

Helen: *Laughs* That's not possible.

Terry: Do you have a box with his stuff in it? He's calling something "The Box".

Helen: That's his ashes.

Terry: Oh. He's in a box. Oh. I thought maybe he was in an urn.

Helen: No.

Terry: He's in a box. Alright. That's why he calls it "The Box".

Helen: Yes.

Terry: Alright. He just touched me which they're only supposed to do if they either want to convey how they passed, which we already know and thank you for not letting me feel that, but the other rule is you can't just touch me during the reading.

He doesn't care. He got excited. That's all he did, like, "Yes!" Okay.

Helen: What we do is we take ashes and we go on a trip.

Terry: No wonder why he's always there.

Helen: So he went to Puerto Rico with us and we put him in the water over there. I'm taking him to Spain. I took him to Colorado.

Terry: That's funny. He's saying, "You know, that's nice for you guys". He's there anyway, but that's nice because his ashes are giving you comfort. Did someone make jewelry out of it? Did someone talk to you about doing jewelry?

Helen: Yes. I don't know if they did it, but yes.

Terry: Because this is what he's talking about also. Oh my God. Alright. So…

Helen: He's really loud. He wasn't going to come through.

Terry: Really? Why wouldn't your son come through?

Helen: You said that someone you think about won't come through.

Terry: Normally they don't because you're thinking about them and when you think you create heavy energy. Were you thinking about starting to walk in fields or by streams or trees? Because your son is trying to put you in the country. He calls it a country, but you need to go where it's peaceful.

Helen: That would be me.

Terry: Okay. What is he speaking of?

Helen: Forests and the beach.

Terry: Okay. It's very peaceful. He goes there. It's very peaceful, and he likes that. Who feeds the birds?

Helen: I do.

Terry: Okay. So he just wants to reconfirm that he wants you there. Okay? Are there doves where you are?

Helen: Yeah.

Terry: Okay. Feed them, he's saying.

Helen: I feed the pigeons in the morning at the train station.

Terry: Okay. It's so funny. You ready? Remember the Holy Spirit? It comes in as a dove. You know a pigeon is a dove. It is when you're in that action of sending nourishment to God's creatures that you're at peace. It might only last a minute or two. That's why he's saying go there and feed the doves. He's touching me. Who has or had the nervous energy? I'm rubbing my fingers. This is what I'm doing. Or I could be counting. One, two, three, four, five. He's looking at you.

Helen: It's Tyler. Tyler's always fidgeting.

Terry: Who's Tyler?

Helen: Tyler's my son.

Terry: His brother. Okay. So he's mentioning his siblings a little bit one by one.

Helen: Yes. He is.

Terry: Because you have to know it's him, he's saying. "You have to know it's me."

Helen: He's very anxious.

Terry: What?

Helen: My son, Tyler, is very anxious. Yeah.

Terry: If you put the color green in his room - it could be part of the bedspread or it could be just a piece of material with green and you put it under the bed between the mattress and the box spring. On the other side colors have their own vibrational energy attached to them. Green is always healing. That's why it's not a coincidence that if you have a hard time sleeping, they'll say put sage, like the color sage, or green. That's Archangel Rafael, by the way. He didn't bring in the archangel. Michael is the only one he hangs out with. But something is so unfair. Something is going on. He's not speaking of his passing. Something going on and I think the energy of it affects you. It's unfair. He keeps saying, "Tell my mom it's unfair". Again, he's not speaking of his passing because that would be unfair. It's a situation going on near you. It's unfair. Don't try to apply logic to it. It's unfair. He points to my refrigerator. Is someone having a problem with a refrigerator or a kitchen appliance?

Helen: My oven isn't working.

Terry: Okay. So he knows this. He's going to kind of stop messing with you.

Helen: That would be nice. He's been really messing with me, apparently.

Terry: Yeah. Are you like putting things down and then…

Helen: Yes. And he opened all my mother's drawers the other day. Opened it.

Terry: Yeah. OCD.

Helen: He's never done that before. Why is he doing that this week?

Terry: Because he wants your attention. Everyone is saying, "I need signs that you'll be there," or, "Give me a sign that you're okay". You can't tell him what kind of signs to do. So that's what he's doing. But he was laughing at the door.

Helen: At the door.

Terry: If he could have, he would have filmed it and put it on YouTube, he's saying. That's how funny it was.

Helen: It was ridiculous.

Terry: He wants me to explain the difference between a dream and a visit. You may know the difference, but he has told me. A dream you're going to forget when you wake up. A visit comes during the dream state not to scare you. When you wake up, you're going to think that just happened. And you'll never forget it until the end of your life. He comes like the visits because even though he made fun of you at the door, if you opened the door and saw him standing there, you'd have a heart attack.

Helen: I would have.

Terry: You think not. Let me tell you something, you think not. And everyone says, "Oh, I wish I had this gift. I wish I had the gift". Remember what I said at the beginning. Gifts are curses as well. So for someone like me who has been doing this for so long, up until sixteen, I was cool. You can read in my first book, it's called the Leona Drive devil. Okay? That was the first time I actually saw evil and had to deal with evil. Why? Because I had to know the difference. None of you know the difference and that's why he brings Archangel Michael to you. He's the protector. Now the other thing you can do to protect yourself is picture three hula hoops. Again, I'll draw a little stick figure. It's just a visualization or you can get a piece of paper and do the colors in strips, as I say. The hula hoop furthest away from you is purple. Why? When Archangel Michael is actively protecting us, the aura from his sword turns purple. He wears blue - dark blue, but when he's protecting us, the aura from the sword is purple. So if you feel something and you get a little nervous, picture the three hula hoops. And it works because colors have energy on the other side. And energies that come through the purple will not be heavy, dark, negative, or evil. They just won't be able to do anything. The next hula hoop is green. That's always healing. Green is Archangel Rafael. The healing could be for yourself or someone else. It could be physical, mental, emotional, or spiritual healing either for you or someone else. The hula hoop you can never take off is white. That comes from the light of God. So now with this piece of paper, Mom, he's saying, "You could give her a choice, but I know what she's going to do". You may keep it or you discard it. The way to discard it is you put it over a sink and put a match to it, but you only burn a corner because you don't want to start a fire. Just thank God for allowing the loved ones to come through, then put a lot of water on it. Then you can throw it out. And then I promised God that anyone I read I would ask when they find themselves totally alone to offer three very informal prayers. The informal prayers are all for people living. They pray for us because we're in hell. There are levels of hell, but we're in hell. So informal prayer said by the heart. It's only a sentence or two. So you have to feel it, not just recite it. So it's for someone you care about who's alive, someone you don't even know because we have lost souls here, or someone you know who is a lost soul and someone you know and you don't like them or trust them.

A Letter From Helen

☆ ★ ☆ ★ ☆ ★ ☆ ★

My mom, Ana Lydia, has a "gift". Right before any grandchild is born, her Ancestors will present her with the baby. So right before Brian was born, she told me she was canceling her trip to Atlantic City. I told her there was no need because Brian was not due until June twenty-sixth. Her trip was only one day, but she really believed that Brian would be born that week. She was one hundred percent right. Brian was eager to come to this world and was born on June 6th, 1990; twenty days before his due date.

On October 2nd, 1993, I had a dream of Brian. He was just three years old. We were dancing together and everything was full of joy and happiness. Brian loved music and dancing. When I was watching the kids, we would blast music while cleaning and we'd dance. But in this dream, the music stopped and his eyes were not bright at all. I wrote the dream on a little piece of paper.

October 2, 1993

My Dear Brian,

I dreamt of you tonight. Something tells me that your future will have a lot to do with dancing. In the dream, while I was giggling, you actually looked at me. These eyes, with great power, looked back at me. Although you were small, you were still able to dip me. But one thing that really concerned me and made me wake up was that beautiful twinkle in your eyes wasn't there and I immediately felt old and wanted to just grab you once again.

I love you, my dear Brian.

Helen

I wrote the experience on a piece of paper. I kept the dream in a little piece of paper and held onto it all this time. It left me in tears when I later realized it was a premonition of the worst thing that would happen to all of us. No matter how many times I told that dream, I could never stop it, ever.

The first time Brian got lost, he was only five years old. We went to an event at Clason Point where there were a lot of people. When I turned around, he was gone. My heart dropped. I went crazy looking for him. They announced his name on stage. I was so angry and happy to see him.

He got lost again; this time at a walk-a-thon in Central Park. He decided to walk ahead of us and we would meet at the finish line. By the time we got to the finish line, he was not there, and all I thought was, *Oh my God. Here we go again*. Mind you, he was already in his teens, but I still freaked out. Found him. He was alright, pretty much saying, "Mom, I'm good. Don't worry". The last time we played hide and seek like that was on the day he died.

In high school, I feared he would not find any friends. I was wrong. He had a lot of friends. They were like him. When Theresa described Brian as a bit of a misfit, she was right. All of his friends still keep in touch with one another. He loved to play jokes with them and hang out.

On August 15th, 2014, he made plans with his brother, Tyler, to go to the beach in Atlantic City after they repaired the elevator. I received the phone call from Tyler that something happened and was told to get there really fast. I called my sister, Annie, and my neighbors, Janet, Kathy and Nanny. We got everyone in a car and headed over there.

That's when he got lost for the third time. By the time we got to the scene, his body was gone. We were told to go to the morgue. He wasn't there, so we went to the hospital. It was messed up. All I kept thinking was, Brian is messing around again. Even after death, I was chasing after him.

Jersey would not let me see son. I begged and they would not do it. Until I saw him for myself, I wouldn't believe it. I called Ortiz Funeral home, and they agreed to pick up the body and bring him to the Bronx. Another fight with the funeral home. When his body was released, I wanted to see him. The funeral home refused. My sister and I insisted. Finally, after waiting four days, I walked in the room with my sister Annie and daughter Elyce. The father was also there. I decided to turn on Pandora, not knowing which song would come on. The song, This Will Be The Day That I Died, played on my phone. Elyce and Annie were angry at me, but there are no coincidences. Life is funny and weird at times. My my Miss American Pie.

Theresa, after Brian died, all of us had visits from Brian. We all reacted the same way. When you told me that if you were to open the door and see him you would faint, all of us had a dream just like that. I opened the door to exit a room and I saw Brian. My first reaction was to ask, "What are you doing here? You're supposed to be dead". Her daughter, Gwendolyn, also had a dream of Brian. She opened the door and was surprised to see him and said the same thing. "What are you doing here? You're supposed to be dead." A friend from high school also had a similar experience. I never told him about the dream, but when he said to me his reaction was to say, "What are you doing here? You're supposed to be dead," I knew it was a visit from Brian. He was much taller and looked iridescent and handsome. He put his arms around my shoulders to protect me and I felt safe again in his arms.

SEVEN

☆ ★ ☆ ★ ☆ ★ ☆ ★

Someone once asked me why I share my gift with others, considering how often I'm judged for being gifted. If you read my first book, you understand how many times people tell me I'm going to hell for what I can do. But that no longer bothers me because I love being able to help people heal through the messages I'm able to pass along. I can see the comfort when their loved ones come through; even through their tears. You can feel the weight come off them. They are still in mourning, but they are okay now, not just wondering if they are. I am truly blessed to be able to help people heal this way.

Even though I've spoken to spirit almost all my life, I am still learning. Sometimes, during a reading, I learn new signs or new meanings to signs I already know. Sometimes when I'm doing a reading for someone else, I'm lucky enough to get answers to questions I have about my own life. Like this next reading. A gentleman explained to me that he was the reason I wasn't able to finish the book up until this point in time.

☆ ★ ☆ ★ ☆ ★ ☆ ★

∞ The Story of Eight ∞

Danielle's Reading

☆ ★ ☆ ★ ☆ ★ ☆ ★

Terry: Okay. Pencils are there. Choose a pencil. Rub it between both hands and then you can just shoot it down to me. Roll it down. So you know the first portion of the read consists of them reciting three different months. These different months could either be directly associated with someone who has passed or someone living to show me the chain of attachment to you. The month of August. What does either any day in August, the eighth of any month, or the number eight mean to you?

Danielle: My father just passed in August.

Terry: Oh sorry. I'm sorry. The big one, this is the reason you're here. Big one is written. Oh God. Wait a minute. You don't mean just last month?

Danielle: August, yeah. This August.

Terry: No. Did you ask for an appointment after he passed?

Danielle: Mm hmm.

Terry: Wow. Sorry.

Danielle: It's okay.

Terry: But he's not suffering. And he's not being quiet on the other side. He had a few people to look up when he was on the other side - to talk to.

Danielle: Yeah. Oh yeah.

Terry: And then he let it go. See, there was something with someone on the other side that I don't know whether it bothered him still when he was in body form, but the person was already on the other side and he was just carrying it around with him like, "Where am I going to put it? Where am I going to put it?"

Danielle: Yeah.

Terry: So when he passed whatever that was that attached him to this other person on the other side is now forever gone.

Danielle: It's gone?

Terry: Yeah.

Danielle: I know what it is.

Terry: You know what he's talking about?

Danielle: Yes.

Terry: Okay. That's fine because he pulls down a black curtain. When they pull down a black curtain, he doesn't want me to get any further confirmation. He wants the details to stay between father and daughter.

Danielle: Yeah.

Terry: So I'm going to let him do that.

Danielle: Okay.

Terry: The month of April. What does either any day in April, the fourth of any month, or the number four mean to you?

Danielle: I'm the fourth of July. That's my birthday.

Terry: Okay. Alright. So Dad came here to see you. Okay. That's cool. And your last month is November. What does any day in November, the eleventh of any month, the number eleven, mean to you? Hold on. *Pencil scratching paper* You know they never show me bad. I just have to write this.

Danielle: There are a couple of things. I'm not sure.

Terry: Okay.

Danielle: November is his brother's birthday. That would be the issue with the other side.

Terry: There you go. Okay. That's what he's speaking of.

Danielle: I think that's it because there was bad blood at the end. His brother passed first.

Terry: Yes. There you go.

Danielle: But, also, it rings a bell to September eleventh, which is a connection.

Terry: Why?

Danielle: He had health issues from that.

Terry: So it's both. Okay.

Danielle: So I'm not sure which eleven.

Terry: It could be both. Okay. One sign can have a few different meanings because it saves them energy, so they're going to rely on my ability to read them.

Danielle: I'm sorry. November was his brother and the eleventh is September eleventh.

Terry: Okay. That's fine. He's touching my heart. Did he have heart issues?

Danielle: Yes.

Terry: Okay. Doesn't have to be the way he passed, but he would have had to suffer from it.

Danielle: That's right.

Terry: He had heart issues, but, "That's not what got me".

Danielle: No.

Terry: The little house in Connecticut, or the house in Connecticut. Was someone speaking about moving to Connecticut or getting a summer home near the lake? He's checking out Connecticut, he's saying.

Danielle: Connecticut?

Terry: Yes.

Danielle: Oh, I don't know. Um.

Terry: Does someone live in Connecticut? Was there a family member? He's checking out Connecticut. There's going to be a connection to Connecticut.

Danielle: Okay.

Terry: So if someone is saying they want to get a summer home and they're looking elsewhere, they may want to look at Connecticut. So who is the person who was saying?

Danielle: We had something in the summer, but it wasn't Connecticut.

Terry: No.

Danielle: Oh. This is someone looking.

Terry: Yes. Exactly. He makes me feel like someone is having a conversation. This is a current event. It's not a memory, he's saying. Like, listen, why don't we, maybe for the summer, go to the lake? He's telling you to go to Connecticut for this. Whenever you hear this conversation, you may want to interject with that.

Danielle: Okay.

Terry: Living. Someone has tired blood right now. Who's that?

Danielle: Like anemic?

Terry: Yeah. That's tired blood.

Danielle: That's me.

Terry: Okay. Alright. Is someone acting out in the state of Florida?

Danielle: There's a connection to Florida.

Terry: What's the connection to Florida?

Danielle: He has a house there, my dad.

Terry: Is there trouble near that house or are people... Because he writes trouble? Just so you see *show's paper* this says "Trouble. Florida". Okay? Now I have to figure out why. Is it legal matters that he's speaking about?

Danielle: Yeah. I think with the house. I think there are issues there with the house that he owns.

Terry: Oh. Okay. There's trouble there. Not that someone is getting in trouble. That's all that he is trying to tell me. Who had the scar on the face?

Danielle: Oh my God. That's my... Is he showing you... That could be me.

Terry: Why?

Danielle: He does too; from our dog. We both have it.

Terry: Oh. Okay. There you go. So the scar on the face is for both of you. Okay. *Looks at Danielle's face* I can't see the scar. And here's the other thing. It's written in pen. Anything in pen was written before your arrival.

Danielle: Oh my God.

Terry: So he's okay. You're not. And he's saying don't run away from the pain. You have to work through it. And you have a girl?

Danielle: Two girls.

Terry: You have two girls.

Danielle: Yeah.

Terry: Did you want another child?

Danielle: Yeah.

Terry: I think you're going to get a boy soon.

Danielle: Well, now I don't think I could have another baby, but if I could, I probably would.

Terry: Oh.

Danielle: It's funny. I just had a conversation with my husband a couple of nights ago that for some reason I never wanted a third, but I feel this need to have a boy.

Terry: So he's repeating a conversation he heard. When did you have that conversation?

Danielle: Just a few nights ago.

Terry: Okay. That's when Dad arrived for this reading.

Danielle: Oh my God.

Terry: So they don't just come on the day of the reading. Well, for me they'll come on the day of the reading, but for you, they visit you every day, but in particular the moment of that conversation is when he stayed with you twenty-four seven. From that moment on; to get ready for this reading with you. Which he's shocked he's even doing this. He said, "Hey listen. I don't even know how I got here, why I'm doing this because all you people are crazy".

Danielle: Terry, he never liked when I came to you.

Terry: Really? Oh my God, he used to know you came here. Isn't that funny?

Danielle: And he didn't like it.

Terry: Well, what are you wasting your money for? *Laughs* Wow. Yeah. That's what he's saying. "I don't know how I even got here."

Danielle: I figured I'd give it a shot. I knew.

Terry: He's going near his throat. Why? Did they have to intubate him?

Danielle: Yes.

Terry: He didn't like that. That was the last nail for him. He was done. Who's Joe on the other side? Not living.

Danielle: Um, oh on the other side?

Terry: Yeah. I know there's a Joe living.

Danielle: Yeah.

Terry: Not that I know, because he tells me. So he does this. So when someone crosses their fingers, he's saying one is with him and one is here, but he doesn't want to go to the one here yet. Meaning living. He wants to go to the one over there.

Danielle: It has to be like an older...

Terry: No. It's not even older because he's telling me it's an equal generation to Dad. Generation is ten to fifteen years, but what he's telling me is someone could have passed - let's say his father passed - but around the age your father did then he would come in as equal to me. So this Joe is on the other side. The brother tried crossing him over. He wasn't ready for that. He said, "Go get someone else. I'm not leaving". I'm telling you. He was dead set that he was going to straighten this brother out when he was on the other side.

Danielle: Yeah.

Terry: So he said, "I'm not leaving with you. You know what, just leave me here then unless you bring someone else." And Joe came.

Danielle: Oh my God.

Terry: Who was Joe? Joe, Joey, Joseph. Did he have a friend?

Danielle: Oh yeah. He did.

Terry: On the other side?

Danielle: Yeah. I think he passed away a few years ago.

Terry: There you go.

Danielle: Yeah. He was that age. Yeah.

Terry: So Joe came. Joe wasn't supposed to cross him over. His brother was. Your father said, "Nope. Then you know what? Leave me here. I'm not going with you". He was pissed.

Danielle: Yeah.

Terry: Not that he was passing because he was grateful that was going to be over with, but because of all people they sent his brother. He said, "No. I'm not going with him. No. Send me someone else".

Danielle: But it's settled now?

Terry: Now it's settled because remember during passing you're still human. You're not a spiritual being. His friend Joe came. So he just wants you to know Joe crossed him over. Okay. Does someone drive a Ford?

Danielle: Yeah.

Terry: Is it a white Ford or a light colored Ford? He's talking about the Ford.

Danielle: Well, my husband drives a Ford.

Terry: It's not a light colored Ford.

Danielle: No.

Terry: Okay. Was he going to get another car?

Danielle: We want to get another car; a Ford.

Terry: Okay. You may want a white one or a light one, he's saying.

Danielle: Yeah. I like the white one.

Terry: There you go. That's what he thinks you should get. He said, "I'm just saying. You don't have to listen to me. But you're good. You do listen," he says.

Danielle: I do.

Terry: Yeah. That's what he says. My neck also started hurting me. I still think this is Dad because he's really not letting anyone else in.

Danielle: Okay.

Terry: So I have pain from here to here. Did you ever see him complain about it, or did he ever try to touch his neck anywhere?

Danielle: Yeah. He had cysts and what not from lymphoma in his neck.

Terry: Oh.

Danielle: That's from 9/11.

Terry: Oh, really. I hope you guys got compensated for it. Not that that makes it easier. I know it doesn't.

Danielle: No.

Terry: I know.

Danielle: No, but yeah.

Terry: Okay. That's okay. He does love February. Who's February?

Danielle: Um.

Terry: So when they write the month on the top of the page as opposed to down here, that means just go to the month. Don't say anything else.

Danielle: There are a lot of birthdays in February.

Terry: Whomever it is, he's sending a lot of love there.

Danielle: Wow. Yeah. That makes sense.

Terry: Okay. My ears, this is someone living. It may even be one of your daughters. I don't know. So I felt pressure in my ear. Is one of them suffering from ear aches? Infections?

Danielle: Not so much infections, but there's a lot going on there.

Terry: Yeah. There's a lot of fluid because I feel pressure in my ear and it's affecting the hearing. Not permanently. And you know they never show me bad. As a matter of fact, if they do speak about something medical for someone in body form, the ending is good.

Danielle: Okay.

Aha Moment: Some time after the reading Danielle sent me a message.

"My daughter had an ear infection at this time and we didn't know until it got really bad."

Terry: Okay. "You need to have the home", he's saying. Were you selling your house?

Danielle: No. We were thinking about it.

Terry: Okay. So I think it's going to be you with the summer home.

Danielle: Really?

Terry: I do. I do.

Danielle: Oh my God. I know what he's talking about.

Terry: Oh. Okay.

Danielle: I can't believe I forgot about this. My mother and I were looking at Airbnb to go for his one-year anniversary from when he passed to a house in Connecticut near the beach.

Terry: There you go. On the beach. He'll be there.

Danielle: It was a lake. A small, little lake in front of the house. Right there.

Terry: There you go.

Danielle: I forgot about that.

Terry: You forgot. He didn't. Because he can hear everything. Now, he said, "I would play with her a little and say I could read her mind," but he can't. It's when you speak of him or think of him that he knows it's okay for him to listen to this conversation. That's what he's saying. Okay. He has the dog. This dog passed old though because for the dog I see gray. Is this your dog? Or was this his dog?

Danielle: Oh yeah. It was our dog.

Terry: Okay. He's so happy. He would have never thought. He had a friend, it could have been a friend or a business associate, of Asian descent. Did you ever hear him speak about either a Chinese person or a Japanese person?

Danielle: A friend?

Terry: Or a business acquaintance. And he's on the other side.

Danielle: Okay.

Terry: Because he even saw him. And the guy, believe it or not, even though I see that he's of Asian descent, he goes by an American name like Mike, Mikey.

Danielle: Okay.

Terry: So just keep that in mind.

Danielle: It could have been a coworker.

Terry: It could have been. I don't know. But he died young. So this gentleman was there. Um, it's probably going to be a new floor. Was someone speaking about getting a new floor or was I thinking, let me get rugs? Your father is saying, "It's probably going to be a new floor". Could he be speaking about Mom's place?

Danielle: No. In our basement we were thinking about putting new…

Terry: Oh. "It's got to be a new floor", he's saying. Do you know the name Donna?

Danielle: Yes.

Terry: How do you know Donna?

Danielle: That's one of my best friends.

Terry: Okay. There's an answer to a prayer going to her. Just to let her know. Donna is written in pen up here.

Danielle: Oh my gosh.

Terry: So he's saying hi to Donna. Who smokes the pot?

Danielle: Like pot? Like marajuana?

Terry: Yeah.

Danielle: My cousin.

Terry: Were you just with this cousin?

Danielle: Yeah.

Terry: Okay. There you go. It's the person you were just with or recently with.

Danielle: Yeah.

Terry: Did you get a sweater of his or something that goes over your head?

Danielle: That goes over my head?

Terry: It's either a sweater that can hug you or a sweater that can go over, like a sweatshirt.

Danielle: No. I took something else of his.

Terry: No. He wanted you to have - so you could wear it - a sweater, so if you need to feel your father's arms, it could be the sweater.

Danielle: He must have seen me going through his closet.

Terry: Oh. Okay. And you have his picture with you?

Danielle: Yeah.

Terry: He's saying, "She has my picture. You want to look at it?" Okay. I don't argue with the dead. Can I? And he's saying he's still not used to being referred to like that. He has a few friends there, by the way, hunny.

Danielle: Oh yeah.

Terry: Even a guy named Jimmy. Who is Jim, Jimmy, or James? It's the same name.

Danielle: That's my mother's grandfather that he always liked.

Terry: There you go. So he's here.

Danielle passes Terry a photo

Terry: Oh my God.

Danielle: And they took a picture of us when we were little, but I don't know where it is. It's my favorite picture on the fourth of July. I put that in here, too.

Terry: Who can't grow a plant or take care of a garden?

Danielle: *Laughs* Me.

Terry: Okay. He's going to help you. He's saying, "Listen. Next year when it's time in the beginning you may notice it's going to be the same result or it's going to look as if it's going to have the same results". But it's going to be better because he's going to help you now that he can. It's not you with the bird feeder, right?

Danielle: Yeah.

Terry: Oh. "Get rid of it", he's saying. That's your problem. I'm going to tell you, you may not have known this, but hearing in one ear was off.

Danielle: For my dad?

Terry: Yeah.

Danielle: He had tinnitus.

Terry: Okay. He might be correct. I don't know. Well, I'm sure he's correct. I just don't know. Were you one of the chosen people for my second book?

Danielle: I don't know. He didn't tell me. You?

Terry: I'm writing the second book. It's going to be called, I believe, the Story of Eight. Did I ever reach out to you?

Danielle: No.

Terry: Okay. He wants to be in my book.

Danielle: *Laughs* He would want to be in a book.

Terry: So I'll send you the information. Let me just do this. Today is nine twenty-five. Did he want to be a firefighter?

Danielle: He was always intrigued by that. He was part of the first responding team.

Terry: So what was his profession?

Danielle: He was in construction from when I was little and then when I got older he worked for the city of New York as a construction project manager.

So he worked in New York City. That's why he was down there.

Terry: And Pete is there?

Danielle: I know Pete. My father-in-law is Pete.

Terry: No. This is an equal guy.

Danielle: Oh. That's my mother's cousin, Pete.

Terry: Okay. He wants to come in and say hello. They're taking good care of your dad.

Danielle: They all loved him.

Terry: Okay. He smiles every day. Oh. I got the chills. He smiles every day because he sees you guys every single day. He couldn't take it anymore, he says. "I was tired," he's saying. Are you his only daughter?

Danielle: Yeah.

Terry: Oh my god because the sun rose and set on you. "That's my angel." What is the angel? Okay. Do you have a picture or a statue of an angel?

Danielle: Yes.

Terry: Where is that?

Danielle: Right by him.

Terry: Is it by his picture?

Danielle: Yes.

Terry: Okay. That's why he calls you his angel. "Oh, my angel." Then he says, "Speaking of angels, she has one in the room".

Danielle: So does my daughter.

Terry: Really? Did your life get any easier because it's going to?

Danielle: Mine?

Terry: Yeah. Not easier since he passed, hunny. No. That's not what he means. Things are going to get easier for you.

Danielle: I hope so.

Terry: With a big blue ribbon on it from dad.

Danielle: It's been a rough time.

Terry: I can't even imagine. Well, I can. You're young. How young are you?

Danielle: I just turned forty.

Terry: Okay. So I was fifty when my dad passed. My dad lived with me because he and my mom were divorced and even though it's a natural progression, it's still daddy.

Danielle: Yeah.

Terry: It's still daddy. He is dancing just for the hell of it.

Danielle: He likes to dance.

Terry: Just for the hell of it because normally I will say it either means they used to dance or they're whole again. He said, "No. There's no reason. I don't need a reason. I could be in a supermarket dancing".

Danielle: He dances everywhere all the time.

Terry: He still does. And Linda. Who's Linda?

Danielle: Linda?

Terry: He said, "Mention Linda". Now I don't know where Linda is.

Danielle: I live on Linda Avenue.

Terry: There you go. Okay. He dances in your house then.

Danielle: Well, I was just dancing this morning.

Terry: Oh my God. He was probably dancing with you.

Danielle: So yesterday actually, oh this is so embarrassing to admit, I was alone, by myself, and I was really upset and thinking about him. I was crying because the girls weren't with me, so I was letting it out. I said, "Alexa, play music," and one of his favorite songs came on.

Terry: Not a coincidence.

Danielle: And I danced and I imagined him dancing. I saw him dancing right in front of me.

Terry: Oh my God. Because he was.

Danielle: And I did the dance that he used to do while laughing.

Terry: Oh my God. Because he was.

Danielle: Yeah.

Terry: You know there's no such thing as a coincidence, right?

Danielle: Yeah.

Terry: Did he get a medal for something? Or an award for something?

Danielle: Yeah. For Vietnam. I found a little medal that he had.

Terry: When did you find this medal?

Danielle: After he passed.

Terry: Okay. You have it?

Danielle: Yeah.

Terry: Good. Good. You know, you may want to forget the connection to Jersey. So what's the connection to Jersey? Is there a friend that lives in Jersey? Is there a business opportunity in Jersey?

Danielle: There are some relatives and a friend of mine that live in Jersey.

Terry: So he's saying you may want to forget.

Danielle: Forget it?

Terry: So if these are good friends, that's not what he's speaking of.

Danielle: Oh okay.

Terry: Yeah. No. No. No. No. Could someone have been speaking about maybe there's an opportunity in Jersey? What do you think? And your father is already answering and the answer is no.

Danielle: Someone is connected to Jersey that I could see my father telling me to forget about.

Terry: Okay. So just leave it there.

Danielle: Okay.

Terry: He just gave me - he took them out of a bag because you don't serve them in a bag - you put them in a dish - of peanuts. So when I see peanuts either, that was something he would love.

Danielle: Yeah. Oh yeah.

Terry: Or I could have gone to a nickname, Peanut. The scent. S - C - E - N - T. You smell your father?

Danielle: Yes.

Terry: That's him, but he wants you to know he's not only there when you smell him. "That's the only time I allow you to know I'm there or you would sit down all day just waiting for my arrival. I don't want to feel like I'm rushed," your father is saying. Like, I know I have to be somewhere, but then I have to plan that. I just want to pop in, make sure everything is alright and pop out.

Danielle: I thought I was imagining it.

Terry: No. He's saying tell her the scent is him. He's there. He has a lot of things to say. Do you have an extra room in the house?

Danielle: Yes.

Terry: Okay. Were you thinking of painting it?

Danielle: Yes.

Terry: This is Dad; what color do you think you're going to paint it?

Danielle: I don't know, Dad.

Terry: How old is the little one?

Danielle: She just turned a year.

Terry: You know what hunny? That might be filled with a baby. I don't know. I keep feeling baby.

Danielle: Really?

Terry: Thomas John. Do you know someone either named Thomas John or the initials T.J.?

Danielle: So it could be two things. One, my brother is Thomas, also like my father. Or, I said to my husband that if I was to have a son, it would be Thomas Joseph.

Terry: Oh. T.J.

Danielle: Yeah. And we would call him T.J.

Terry: Alright. Get ready for that.

Danielle: *Laughs*

Terry: One of your mother's "boyfriends", as he calls them, is here. When Mom was younger, because Mom is still with us because I don't feel her there.

Danielle: Yeah. Yes.

Terry: When Mom was young, there was a guy who had a crush on her.

Danielle: Okay.

Terry: And I think there was someone that maybe Dad used to needle her, or it became a joke. No disrespect to the guy. Because he said one of her boyfriends is here. Now, this will not be someone who if your mother found out he passed she would be really upset.

Danielle: Right.

Terry: Because they don't do that stuff. It could have even been an older fellow and your father would tease, "Oh he's your boyfriend". That's why. And who's Tony?

Danielle: He has an Uncle Tony.

Terry: Okay. On the other side, this one is.

Danielle: Oh yeah.

Terry: Okay. He's coming in. The younger one, is she having digestive issues?

Danielle: She did have digestive issues.

Terry: Okay. Someone's door is not working the right way. So I don't know if the lock isn't working the right way. There's something with the door. I think I go more near Mom. Now, who does Mom live with? By herself?

Danielle: She's by herself.

Terry: She's not going to stay like that.

Danielle: No.

Terry: I don't think so.

Danielle: The door, they were going to fix the screen door because it won't shut.

Terry: Maybe you could ask your husband to do that. I think Mom may want to buy a bigger house. So when I say she's not going to stay like that, she's not finding anybody, it's that I want to be with family.

Danielle: Yeah.

Terry: Where does she live right now?

Danielle: They moved just a couple of minutes from me.

Terry: Oh good. So she is close to you.

Danielle: Yeah.

Terry: "She could keep it and she could rent it out if she wants because she's not going to be able to stay there", your father is saying. Not because of financial reasons. It's going to be too much for her because she just goes into one room after the other crying and the memories are going to kill her because she's having it real bad. In a different way. Did he almost pass around someone's birthday?

Danielle: Yes.

Terry: Okay. Go ahead.

Danielle: My baby turned one two days later.

Terry: On the ninth. There you go. He did not want to pass on her birthday. Okay. So yes. He was still there. He was surprised, though. "It's not like Scrooge," he's saying. When you see the movie Scrooge, nothing is scary. He's saying, "If I would have known it was this easy I would have had more fun in body form than I did". Although he did know some characters.

Danielle: Oh yes.

Terry: He did.

Danielle: *Laughs*

Terry: He does not like what's going to be happening here on earth. That's one of the regrets he has. But he feels that if he was here on earth, you would have to take care of him. He wouldn't be able to take care of you and that he doesn't regret. Okay? Even his bowels hurt him.

Danielle: Yeah.

Terry: He's getting real because he said to me, "They told me here on the other side to trust you. I really thought you were a witch and I thought you were taking advantage of my daughter. So I'm glad to meet you from this side." But can I tell you something? My own father did not find out about me until after he passed.

Danielle: What? He didn't know?

Terry: I would never tell him. He never knew and I started seeing them at three. You know who John ████████ is?

Danielle: Yes.

Terry: Okay, so he's on T.V. It was during Christmas time and I was hanging lights. My father lived with me for the last two years of his life. He said, "Theresa, do you believe this son of a bitch is telling people he can talk to dead people?" I said, "You don't believe that, Daddy?" He got mad. He said, "Let me tell you something. If Jesus Christ himself got off the cross and said to me, 'Carmine, it's true', I'd tell him, 'You know what? Get right back on that cross and nail yourself back up, because I know you're full of shit'. Because if that were true, I would have seen my sister Tessie." His sister Tessie died in her twenties. That's who I was named for.

Danielle: I just got the chills.

Terry: Yeah. Me too. My father found out shortly after he passed because I heard something in my room at night and my dogs were crying, crying, crying, crying. I put the light on and I sat up and there was my father.

Danielle: Oh my God.

Terry: Listen to me. God's honest truth. I thought he was going to get mad at me, so I went back down and shut the light and thought, *Oh my God. Don't let him yell at me.* Like he caught me having sex or something. Like that kind of look. So I know where your father is coming from. I think Mom might need oatmeal.

Danielle: Yes. Oh my gosh.

Terry: He's saying.

Danielle: He made sure she had oatmeal every morning.

Terry: Wow. I'm telling you he's very detailed. I mean, you know it's him.

Danielle: Yeah. There is no doubt in my mind.

Terry: Yeah. There isn't any doubt at all. And Rosie.

Danielle: Oh my God, Terry!

Terry: Yeah. He's mentioning Rosie.

Danielle: That's my mother's cousin. I knew she would be up there with him. I knew it.

Terry: Yeah. So he says, "Listen. Tell her to come in. My daughter will say hello. My daughter will say hello to anyone. I know her". Oh, that's what you're going to do? Okay. There's going to be a sound that either escapes from a child's toy or a wind chime, but not when it's windy out. Obviously, if it's windy out, that's why you buy wind chimes. You want to hear those sounds. It's not going to be windy or your girls will not actively be playing with the toy, but it will go off. That's your father telling you, "I'm here now".

Aha Moment: Sometime after the reading Danielle sent me a message.

"My daughters have a puzzle that makes noises. The rooster often goes off when no one is playing with the puzzle, but we are usually together in the living room where it's stored. Also, shortly after this reading, I received a wind chime in the mail as a gift from an old friend that loved my dad. It has a beautiful saying on it to remember people we've lost."

Terry: There should have been, he's telling me, there was a little money in the house.

Danielle: For my mother?

Terry: Yeah.

Danielle: I think so. Yeah.

Terry: Alright. What was different in the wallet? So I feel it's not money. Could it have been a little medal?

Danielle: Yes. I believe he keeps his… He donated blood and I feel like the little thing is in there.

Terry: It's not paper. It's not plastic. It's a thing.

Danielle: Yes. I'm pretty sure.

Terry: Where is the family that would have had five kids?

Danielle: Who has five?

Terry: He said "would have had". Now, either someone only had three left and they lost two.

Danielle: I don't know. I'm trying to think. He was a family of, or wait. Was it my grandmother? Three boys and two girls were a family of five.

Terry: Okay. So who's mother and father? His mother and father or Mom's mother and father?

Danielle: No. Mom.

Terry: Okay. And are they both on the other side?

Danielle: Yeah.

Terry: Okay. Then I can go there. He's very comfortable with your mom's mother and father.

Danielle: Oh yeah.

Terry: That's his mom and dad, he's telling me.

Danielle: Oh yeah.

Terry: He hangs out a lot with them.

Danielle: Really?

Terry: Yeah. Someone's hand straightened out.

Danielle: His did.

Terry: Oh. So what was wrong with his hand?

Danielle: I don't know. From arthritis. When he was in the hospital with the fluids they were giving him, they actually looked better towards the end of his days.

Terry: There you go. The hands actually straightened out, he's saying. What's with Tuesdays? So Tuesdays he makes me feel is a different day of the week from the rest of them. So either someone has off on Tuesdays or someone used to do something in particular on Tuesdays. Or do you go to a restaurant called Tuesdays? He's specific about the day of the week.

Danielle: I'll ask my brother. Maybe it means something to him.

Aha Moment: Sometime after the reading Danielle sent me a message.

"Tuesdays were the day I set aside to have dinner with my mom. I realized this after the reading."

Terry: Okay. Who's Mary or Maryanne?

Danielle: There's a couple of them.

Terry: Living. Not passed.

Danielle: Yeah. There's an Aunt Maryanne.

Terry: Okay. I don't know why he went to visit her.

Danielle: They were very close.

Terry: Okay. Just visit. Equal female to Dad and Mom. She died young, though. Sorry. She passed young. Equal female means the same generation.

Danielle: Okay.

Terry: She died of an illness. You know what's funny, though? Someone has a picture of her when she was younger. You know Little Red Riding Hood?

Danielle: Yeah.

Terry: It's not that color, but it's that kind of cloak. It could also be a robe with a hood. She's connected to the name Angie.

Danielle: Angie is my grandmother.

Terry: Okay. Did your grandmother lose a child very young?

Danielle: She lost a friend.

Terry: How young was the girl when she passed? Do you know?

Danielle: I think she was pretty young.

Terry: Okay. She's there. They had a big banquet for your father and he was eating barbeque spare ribs right off the grill. He's telling me to tell you. Now, was he on a restrictive diet prior to his passing?

Danielle: He put himself on a diet.

Terry: Okay, because he's not on a diet now.

Danielle: So he's eating everything again?

Terry: Yeah. And the corn on the cob.

Danielle: Okay. Because he made many vows and didn't eat things.

Terry: Oh no. He's eating everything. They tell him he doesn't really have a body, but he's not used to not knowing. So they ease you into knowing that you're passed, but it's never like you pass and you're like, "Can you hear me? Oh my God! Sweetheart. Daddy's here". It's not like that. It's like, really? Like a kid in a candy store, that's what your father just told me to tell you. Oh. The candy store. He's saying that it's not a coincidence that he used the candy store.

Danielle: Candy Store?

Terry: Did he know someone that owned a candy store? Was there a neighborhood candy store that he would always visit with you or for you and your brother?

Danielle: I can't think.

Terry: It has to do with the name Nick.

Danielle: Nick?

Terry: Yeah. Nick, Nicky or Nicole because when they're living I won't know the gender.

Danielle: Oh, they're living? This is a neighbor that's living?

Terry: Yes.

Danielle: My husband has a good friend named Nick, who my father loved.

Terry: Okay. Maybe they had a candy store, they used to sell the candy, there's something with that.

> **Aha Moment:** After the reading, Danielle figured out Nick's dad had a deli.

Terry: He's showing me a fire. With the fire, it's always a memory hunny, so either someone almost died in a fire or did. In the house by accident. I'm not saying there's an arsonist. Or someone could have left something on the stove and it could have turned into a fire.

Danielle: My cousin, Gena, had a big fire in her apartment.

Terry: Oh. Okay. So that's what he's speaking of. He said to me, so he's showing off, and he's right. He calls me Miss. Thank God he doesn't call me Ma'am.

Danielle: No. He wouldn't do that.

Terry: He calls me Miss, which is nice.

Danielle: He always did that no matter the age.

Terry: Okay. Wait a minute. Let me check. Yeah. He would have been older than me, so that's why. He said, "Miss. Listen. Remember when you said, 'Now is the time to finish the book?" I've been working on the book for two years. I could not finish it for some reason. There was a block. He said, "Do you know what you were waiting for? Me. And I want my daughter in the book". You write his little life story. I'll send you what you have to do. "I want them to know I'm a skeptic and I thought everybody like you was crazy. But I'll give you this. They may be crazy. I don't know, but my experience with you is pure". He is the only one that's ever thanked me.

Danielle: Oh my God. He would. That's him.

Terry: Oh. Robbie. Robbie. He keeps yelling this name.

Danielle: Robbie?

Terry: Who's Rob?

Danielle: I just know one Rob. My brother, one of his best friends, is Rob. Is this a younger man?

Terry: Well, I know he's living, so I won't know. If they're passed, I'll know.

Danielle: Or my husband has an Uncle Rob.

Terry: No. I'm picking up younger. I don't know why he just yelled Robbie. I don't feel anyone here. *Points to the other side*. It's on this side. Our side. Wouldn't it be funny if your brother's best friend said to your brother, "I think there's something in my house".

Danielle: That's funny.

Terry: Because he yelled, "Robbie".

Aha Moment: Danielle sent me the following message:

"Shortly after the reading, we found out that my husband's Uncle Rob has cancer."

Terry: Oh, and someone has a portable safe.

Danielle: Like one you can move around?

Terry: Yeah.

Danielle: My husband.

Terry: Alright. He wants to know what he thinks he's going to do with that? So you make it easy for the robbers? They can take it out.

Danielle: Yeah.

Terry: Okay. He has an opinion.

Danielle: Oh. That's an understatement.

Terry: Okay, so you know what to do. Say four informal prayers said from the heart. It's a sentence. Maybe two. For someone living you care about, whatever good wish, someone you don't even know because we have lost souls here, or someone you do know who is a lost soul right now, someone you know and you don't like this person or trust this person. The prayer for that one goes something like, "Dear God, let them find their way, just keep them away from me". So wish them well, then create your boundary. And for us as a society to stop abusing, torturing, and killing kids.

Danielle: Okay.

∞ The Story of Eight ∞

A Letter From Danielle

☆ ★ ☆ ★ ☆ ★ ☆ ★

My father, Thomas (Tom/Tommy) ███████, was an amazing human being. He was truly one of a kind. I was aware of how special he was at a very young age. He was my hero, my idol. I adored him with all my heart. As I grew up and learned more about his life and saw how he was with people, my respect for him grew deeper. I was always so proud to have him as a father. I had "the best dad" everyone would say, and I knew it.

My father's life was not an easy one. He grew up in Bensonhurst, Brooklyn in the fifty's and sixty's when doo-wop and gangs filled the streets. In 1969, he was sent to Vietnam for a year. Although it would be a traumatic experience for him, he always said he was "proud to have served his country". After returning home, he dove deep into drugs, as many vets at the time did. Finally, after a few hard years and run-ins with the law, he was sent to rehab, where he thought was the easy way out of jail. It would save his life. There in renaissance in upstate New York, my father found God and a new beginning. He cleaned up and never touched a drug again. Instead, he used his experiences for better or worse to touch the lives of others. I mention this because it's something he never hid from me and my brother or anyone, really. Perhaps that is what made him so appealing to me and others; that he was honest and humble and he never judged.

My father was everyone's dad. He was the uncle my cousins turned to when they needed advice or help. He was the guy his kids' friends would confide in when they couldn't turn to their own parents. But besides being the confidant, he was the life of the party. His appreciation for life oozed from him. His sense of humor was captivating and his optimism contagious. As I write this I am flooded with so many emotions from the memories that fill my head now and all day every day since his passing. How he was the first one on the dance floor at any party (or really just the first one to dance even if there wasn't a dance floor). How he would say hello to anyone anywhere and treat everyone with kindness and respect as if he knew them his whole life. How he would tell stories and jokes like no other. How he could lay in the sun for hours and hours on a beach or just in our yard. How every single time he would go out to the restaurant to eat he would spend the longest out of everyone to look at the menu only to order the same thing every time: Chicken parmigiana. Most of all, though, how he was the "best dad".

The childhood memories are endless. From Yankee games (He was the biggest Yankee fan ever), Coney Island, horseback riding, fireworks on the Fourth of July (my birthday), singing the Twelve Days of Christmas on Christmas Eve, fishing, New Years Eve parties with the family in three small rooms upstairs in my grandmother's apartment dancing to oldies and the music. Oh, the music and the singing. I remember how he taught me how to pray when I was five, and I still say that prayer every night. The pranks and the jokes. And the time he put into building the perfect snowmen.

There are so many wonderful things that he did with us and for us, it is hard to pick just one. But if I had to pick the thing that sticks out the most from my younger years, it would be our once a year trip upstate to Villa Roma, a resort in the Catskills. The first time we went was in 1986. I was five and my brother, Tommy, was one. We went with my grandparents, my dad's parents, for a little weekend trip. That little getaway turned into a family tradition for thirty-four years. He passed the day before we would have gone for our thirty-fifth year. No matter how much my parents struggled financially, he always managed to take us on that trip. We sang. We danced. We played bocce and cards. We grew up there in the mountains. As each year passed by and my brother and I got older, even in the awkward teenage years, we never lost the importance of being together up there as a family. We teased him that he was the "mayor of Villa

Roma". He knew everyone and everyone knew him. He met his best friend up there when we were kids and his family became our family. The laughs were endless. I feel a deep pain in my heart knowing that he will never be up there again with us, but I will continue to go in his honor and memory.

As I got older, I got to relive all those memories I previously mentioned over again through my daughter, Emma. My father retired when Emma was born in 2015 and when I went back to work when she was eight months old, he watched her every day. My mother said it was like watching me and my dad all over again, except this time he was there every moment of the day. He taught her everything about nature. He took her everywhere he could. Emma and her Baba were best friends. I believe she still hears him and feels him with her, for she speaks to him daily.

It's been a struggle to get through each day without him. How can you when everything you see is a reminder of him? I feel him with me. I talk to him constantly.

At the end of September, about seven weeks after his passing, I went to Terry for a reading. As always, I went with an open mind, hoping for my dad to come through, but not expecting it. My father was not thrilled about my medium experiences. He would be intrigued and let me tell him about it, but then say it was "against God and Jesus" to do that.

Well, not only did my dad come through in this reading, but he spoke to Terry for forty-five minutes straight. He even told her that he didn't trust her and thought she was a "witch" but that others on the other side told him he could trust her. That is when he said he wanted to be in her book for having doubted her, but now believing and, let's face it, the man loved some extra attention. That reading was one of the most beautiful experiences of my life. I had my dad back after watching him suffer for six months and not being able to hear his voice due to a tracheostomy and ventilator. He was there with all of his honesty and humor and love. And he did it because he knew I needed it for comfort that he is at peace "dancing every day".

My father worked at Ground Zero as part of the recovery / clean up. He was a construction project manager for the New York City housing and preservation department downtown near the World Trade Center. In 2015, the day after my daughter was born, he was diagnosed with non-Hodgkin's Lymphoma and mild emphysema from Ground Zero. He remained healthy though; always taking good care of himself. In 2019 he developed a heart condition that was managed with medication. Then in January 2021 he contracted Covid. He developed a severe case of Covid pneumonia and landed in the hospital. That, along with the underlying issues, made recovery difficult. Just when we thought he was making an improvement, something happened. We still are unsure as to what exactly. He couldn't breathe. He was intubated on March 7th. March 6th would be the last time I heard my father's voice. "Love you Danielle." I watched the strongest man I know deteriorate in six months and it was the most painful thing I've ever experienced. I know he fought hard. He even said so to Terry, but he was tired and his body couldn't fight any longer. In that hospital room on August 7th, I finally turned to look out the window at the stars and said, "Dear God, please don't make him suffer any longer. I don't want him to be in pain." And in that moment I felt something in me that I cannot explain and when I turned to look back at my father, I saw him take his last breath.

During the preparation of the book, I asked Danielle to review her chapter. She sent me this note.

"I wrote this almost a year ago. It was very therapeutic for me. This is the first time I've read it since I wrote it. I know now, a year later, that he is at peace and re-reading the reading with Terry validates my feelings that his spirit is with me and my family every day."

EIGHT

☆ ★ ☆ ★ ☆ ★ ☆ ★

Some people look forward to the great beyond. The thought of meeting our passed loved ones in Heaven is what helps get them through the trials and tribulations of life on Earth. But what if someone told you your best friend wouldn't be there waiting for you at the pearly gates or whatever you believe heaven or the afterlife to be. That's what happened to one of my clients. If you've read my first book you'll understand that everyone's religion or spiritual belief holds some part of the truth. No one is totally correct and no one is totally wrong, except the person that told my client he would never see his best friend again. After being told this, he was sent to me so I could clear up a few things he needed to know.

☆ ★ ☆ ★ ☆ ★ ☆ ★

Deborah and Cosmo's Reading

★ ☆ ★ ☆ ★ ☆ ★

Terry: Please pick up a pencil. Rub it between both hands and then you're going to hand it to me. Okay. So, what did I get then? *Terry looks at her paper* Hold on a second. Barry. Oh, the equal man. Okay. Before you got here, the month of October came through. What does any day in October, the tenth of any month or the number ten mean? It could be my name, Terry or Theresa, because this is Saint Teresa's month for me, or someone was religious or lived near a church? So why would I hear October during the prayer part? Is it someone's birthday? Someone's anniversary?

Cosmo: Oh yeah. It's a couple of people's birthdays.

Terry: So I need the acknowledgement then because I don't understand why I heard October. Whose birthday?

Cosmo: Deborah's.

Terry: Oh. Happy Birthday.

Cosmo: My father's.

Terry: Is he on the other side?

Deborah: On the other side, yes. He's deceased.

Cosmo: Yeah.

Terry: Yeah. He was here first. So I just want you to see the paper says father energy. So anything in pen came through before you got here. Okay? He's bringing in an equal male to you. So an equal male could be a brother, brother-in-law, friend, cousin. It's someone from the same generation. So why is he telling me, "Tell my son I'm bringing his equal here"?

Cosmo: So that doesn't mean - for October - my sister. Her birthday is in October too.

Terry: Okay. So that's fine. I'm not going there.

Cosmo: I'm just letting you know.

Terry: So Dad came through during the prayer part. And he's saying, "I'm bringing his equal". Did you lose a friend on the other side? Now this is a gentleman that used to have a problem either with drinking or drugs when he was living. He didn't have to pass from that, but he would have had a problem with it.

Deborah: Billy's brother.

Cosmo: What?

Deborah: Billy's brother is your equal.

Cosmo: Billy's brother?

Deborah: Billy's brother had drugs.

Cosmo: Billy ███████.

Deborah: Yes.

Cosmo: Yeah. He's the one that shot my brother.

Terry: He's the one coming in with your father.

Cosmo: Really?

Terry: Yeah. Your father is bringing him in for some reason. He's bringing in your equal, he's saying. Equal means the same generation.

Deborah: As you.

Terry: So generation is ten years. Dad comes in above you because he's in a generation above you.

Cosmo: Why not Joey? He died from drugs.

Terry: Alright. Who knew Pete? Pete can be living. Pete, Petey, Peter, Peterson. As association with the name Peter or Paul. The P's are here. Did anyone of these guys? Alright. Let's keep going. The month of November came through.

Cosmo: Mm hmm.

Terry: What does any day in November, the eleventh of any month…

Cosmo: Um. The guy that my father brought in, his brother, Billy, is one of my good friends, was born in November.

Terry: Okay. There you go. They're showing me who this equal male is.

Deborah: And your father died in November.

Cosmo: And my father died on my friend's birthday.

Terry: Isn't that funny? It's the father who brought in this gentleman. Not a coincidence then. Alright.

Cosmo: She'll explain everything to me when we leave.

Deborah: *Laughs from her chair in the corner*

Terry: You might as well come right here because he has a look on his face like a deer in headlights.

So just explain to me because I need my clarity. This Billy, it was Billy's brother.

Deborah: *Moves to chair next to Cosmo* What was Billy's brother's name?

Cosmo: Bobby.

Terry: Bobby. Okay. How did you know him? What's with this Bobby?

Cosmo: We lived next door to each other for many years.

Terry: Okay.

Cosmo: And before his death, he shot my brother.

Terry: That's who it is. Okay. Because we had a question as to why was he bringing him? Who is this equal male? But then the very next clue gives us - so they confirm it.

Cosmo: What's the next clue?

Terry: The eleven.

Cosmo: Oh, okay.

Terry: November or the eleventh of any month.

Deborah: Yes. Yes. See?

Terry: Okay? I'm living. Who has the drinking problem?

Cosmo: I don't know.

Terry: Or who had the drinking problem? It's around you guys, by the way.

Cosmo: I have a lot of friends at work that have drinking problems. I know that.

Terry: No. I'm going closer. Does one of your sons have a friend near them that has a drinking problem? Because your dad, he's talking about the drinking problem is too close to his family.

Cosmo: Well we were just talking about it because Billy started drinking again. Billy used to have a drinking problem.

Terry: Oh. So this is a current event. You were just having this conversation.

Cosmo: Yeah.

Terry: Oh. So your father knows about the conversation. That's probably why he's repeating it.

Cosmo: Well, Billy was very good friends with my father.

Terry: There you go. Okay. So he considers him family.

Cosmo: Yeah.

Terry: Because he's saying, "It's near my family. Don't go so far away. It's near my family". So there's really nothing you can do about that, he's saying. And the month of February. They only give me three months. What does any day in February, the second of any month...

Cosmo: Well, a good friend of ours is going to have a baby.

Deborah: We got Bambino in February.

Cosmo: And we got Bambino on February sixteenth, it was.

Terry: It could be any day in February.

Cosmo: February we got our dog.

Terry: Was this a rescue dog?

Cosmo: Yes.

Terry: Okay. Then that's where I'm going. That dog sees dead people.

Deborah: He did. I know.

Terry: Oh, you know.

Deborah: Yeah. We used to say, he'd look in the corner and see my mother, he'd see my grandfather.

Terry: He sees your father. He sees your father too. Your father is in the house.

Cosmo: Oh really?

Terry: Your father's bringing in a woman who's equal to him, so that means in his generation.

Cosmo: My mother.

Terry: Okay. She wants to come in. Did she have any leg problems, walking problems, hip problems, swelling with the legs? There's something with the legs.

Cosmo: I don't know.

Terry: Okay. And she wants me to mention April. So, what does any day in April…

Cosmo: My daughter's birthday.

Terry: Okay. She's just showing me a bloodline. That's all she's showing me. Your daughter, how old is your daughter?

Cosmo: Twenty-eight.

Terry: Okay. So the young girl, this mother before you got here was telling me there are tears of a clown around her. That means I put on a happy face, but I'm suffering inside about something. So who's this young girl? Like I put on a happy face. This does not mean mental illness or something. It just means I'm not the type to talk about what's bothering me. If it's not his daughter, there is a young woman around that has tears of a clown, they're telling me.

Cosmo: I don't know.

Deborah. Yeah. I have two sons.

Terry: No. I know you have the boys. Okay.

Cosmo: Well, it's not her trying to reach out to me because I haven't talked to her in a while.

Terry: Oh. So you may hear. Oh okay. So that makes a little sense. Then she doesn't tell you her business. So your father is just telling you. Or your mother mentioned April, so that's your daughter. So with this young girl, because twenty-eight is young for me, there are tears of a clown there. So I present myself one way, like, happy or I got it together, but meanwhile the exact opposite is true. You may hear some stuff. And they never show me bad, so don't worry about it. Oh shit. Your *Deborah* mom is here. Not "oh shit" that your mom is here.

Deborah: No. I didn't take it that way.

Cosmo: I knew she was going to show up.

Terry: Well, she said she needs to.

Cosmo: She always does.

Terry: Because I need to explain my daughter to you. Not you. You're saying I hate when they do this shit. Your sister.

Deborah: Which one?

Terry: The one that lives with you.

Deborah: Okay. Dawn.

Terry: She's a prisoner of her own thoughts.

Deborah: You understand that?

Cosmo: Absolutely.

Terry: It goes beyond OCD.

Cosmo: Oh.

Terry: But for some reason, she wants to explain that to you.

Cosmo: To me?

Terry: Yeah. She's not making excuses for her daughter. I'm just giving you the reasons why certain things happen.

Deborah: Oh yeah. She's got a lot of...

Terry: Okay. She has a lot of shit going on. It's affecting your sons. It's so funny because your mother says, "I don't want to say the cancer word, but it's like an illness that's affecting everyone in the family." The problem is, it's an illness, so it's not...

Deborah: Going to go away.

Terry: Yeah. Yeah. So your mother's apologizing for this, but she loves her daughter.

Deborah: Of course.

Terry. Because she's saying deep down she's a good person, it's just that it's getting worse.

Deborah: She has issues.

Terry: Yeah, but she's not dealing with them because your mother is saying she's almost like a dry drunk. Meaning it's always someone else's fault. You know?

Deborah: Okay.

Terry: Who's Greg? Gary. Greg. Gary.

Cosmo: Well, I use Craig, but my real name is Cosmo.

Deborah: Everybody knows him as Craig.

Terry: Oh.

Cosmo: Everybody knows me as Craig.

Deborah: His first name was Cosmo.

Terry: Oh. Alright. So that's probably why your mother is using it.

Cosmo: Yeah, because she hated Cosmo. My father named me because I have a twin brother. They took turns. He named me and she named my brother.

Terry: Oh. Isn't that funny? Okay. Joseph is here. I have a Joseph coming through.

Cosmo: A young Joseph?

Terry: Yes. Who is young Joe? Who is this?

Cosmo: ███████.

Deborah: Your friend?

Cosmo: Yeah. He died in 2001.

Terry: Okay. Because your mother is saying, "Tell my son Joseph is here".

Cosmo: Wow.

Terry: So it's okay. Um, so this is what both of these mothers are doing. Don't react. Let me just tell you the movie they're playing, okay? I'm not selling my house, but I'm getting money out of my house. It could be a refinance. Let me just finish. And I see two presents with bows on them with money in it. Because this is what I'm doing. This is for you; it goes to your dad. This is for you; it goes to your sister. And I do this. Eventually what I think is going to happen is the father and sister will not be living there, but they're compensated for not living there. Do you know what I mean?

Deborah: Yes.

Terry: Okay. Just to keep that in the back because she never wants them out on the street.

Deborah: Yeah, I know.

Terry: But if you put like, you know, I gift them money, then it would be alright because it's going to start affecting this, and that's not what your mother wants. It's too much for you. Plus, her energy, even though you're telling me the thyroid is fine and everything, she recently had a scare. Her energy is still low. So this is your mother-in-law talking to you. Okay? Was it your dad who was the drinker? I have a drinker coming through.

Cosmo: My mother.

Terry: Oh. Okay.

Cosmo: My father didn't drink at all.

Terry: Okay. Because the drinker is written in pen. Anything in pen came in before you guys even got here. So Mom was here with Dad. See, here's the father's energy. She's directly under the father's energy. My head started hurting me. So when my head hurts, who either had - now remember, it doesn't have to be the way I passed. I would have had to suffer with it. - either an injury to the head, stroke, aneurysm, alzheimer's, dementia.

Cosmo: Well, there's your son.

Terry: No. This is on the other side.

Cosmo: Oh. Well, our dog just died from a stroke.

Terry: Get out.

Cosmo: Two weeks ago.

Terry: Aw. There you go. There you go. I should have gone before I went, this dog is making me feel. You know when you're on the other side you can communicate because it's not with words. It's only with thoughts. So he's thankful. He's not saying you should have put me down sooner, but he was lucky he made it that far, he makes me feel. Why is he telling me that?

Deborah: Maybe he was older than we thought. He was a rescue.

Terry: Oh. Okay.

Deborah: But we saw him slowing down over the summer.

Terry: Oh. Okay.

Cosmo: We had him for nine years.

Terry: You did. Okay. Prior to his passing, was there a moment or time he should have passed? That's what he makes me feel.

Cosmo: Well, remember when he started acting differently? He started going to the bathroom in the house.

Deborah: Yeah.

Terry: There you go.

Deborah: Which was not like him.

Cosmo: And then he wouldn't stay in the same room. He would go into another room and avoid us.

Deborah: He was distancing himself.

Terry: There you go. Because he knew he was sick. See, when an animal knows it's sick, it won't intermingle with family. It just wants to be almost like a cat. Cats go off on their own to pass. But, he's saying don't feel bad about it. He's having a great time. He's chewing on a T-Bone steak.

Deborah: Told you he's there.

Terry: He's chewing on a T-Bone steak.

Deborah: All dogs go to heaven.

Terry: Anything that grows has a soul, so it's in heaven. Even trees. Because heaven is like three feet above us, but at a much higher vibrational rate. So, like I know my dad is on the other side. His home was his home in the Bronx. I know he's living in a place that looks just like the Bronx home, like when he was there when he was younger. So

anything that grows has a soul. It doesn't have a
heart. It doesn't have blood, but it has a soul. That's
why the American Indians are so into nature.

Deborah: So he didn't suffer.

Terry: No.

Cosmo: He died with us.

Deborah: Do you feel better now?

Cosmo: Absolutely.

Deborah: I told you.

Terry: Oh. Is this why you came here? For the dog?

Cosmo: Yup.

Deborah: Because someone told him that dogs
don't go to heaven...

Terry: Who said that?

Cosmo: I went to a Pastor.

Deborah: ...and that when he dies, he won't be
reunited with the dog.

Terry: Absolutely wrong.

Deborah: *Turns to Cosmo* I told you. My mother had the cat by her feet the last time I came here.

Terry: Oh my God. Are you kidding me? Let me tell you something...

Cosmo: That's what he told me.

Terry: I don't give a shit. A pastor? That should tell you. I went to test out this medium in a group reading so it wasn't just me. He came right up to me and said, "Your rottweiler is right next to you".

Cosmo: Really?

Terry: I said, "Yeah, I know. My J.J." His name was J.R. I called him J.J. for a nickname.

Cosmo: Hey. J.R.

Terry: Get out.

Cosmo: My father's name.

Terry: Isn't that funny? So I'm telling this story. There you go.

Cosmo: So he's not with us now, right?

Terry: Yeah. He's right with you.

Cosmo: The dog is?

Terry: Yeah.

Deborah: See.

Cosmo: Oh.

Terry: And he's going to make himself known, but he's a little skittish about jumping on the bed. So was he not allowed on the bed?

Deborah: Oh he was allowed on the bed, but I think towards the end he was having a hard time getting up so we'd have to coax him.

Terry: So you're going to have to coax him. Not that he can't do it, but he doesn't want to break any rules. So what's going to happen is when you're sleeping you might feel it. I hope you let the new dog sleep on the bed too, right?

Deborah: She misses him like crazy.

Terry: Yeah.

Deborah: We give her a lot of love, but she misses him.

Terry: Okay, but she doesn't go on the bed, right?

Deborah: She doesn't want to.

Terry: Good.

Cosmo: Yeah. She won't. Because they stayed in bed together all day. So she stays out on the couch now.

Deborah: She won't come in.

Terry: Okay. So I'm going to tell the dog to let the other dog know that he's there.

Deborah: Oh. It would make her happy.

Terry: Yeah. But the reason I was asking if the new dog goes on the bed is because you're going to feel a dog on the bed. I don't want it to be the one you actually have in physical form. This one will go on the bed. So it's a male? Medium size?

Cosmo: Big dog.

Deborah: Yeah, he was like ninety pounds.

Cosmo: He was a Pitbull.

Terry: Oh nice. Pitbull.

Deborah: The sweetest.

Terry: And he's showing me a darker dog.

Cosmo: That's what we have.

Deborah: That's what we have.

Cosmo: We have another Pitbull.

Deborah: A black one.

Terry: Oh. There you go. That's why I'm getting confused.

Cosmo: We have a blue nose at home. They've been together for a little more than three years.

Deborah: She misses him.

Terry: She'll start feeling better.

Deborah: Good.

Terry: She's going to start feeling better. What's with you and trucking?

Cosmo: I'm a garbage man.

Terry: Oh. Where?

Cosmo: As a matter of fact, I work up here in Brewster.

Terry: Do you?

Cosmo: Over in Putnam Lake.

Terry: Oh. Wow. Isn't that funny?

Cosmo: I'll come by for a coffee one day.

Terry: Okay. Let me know. My son-in-law is in sanitation in the Bronx; Country Club.

Cosmo. Really? I've been doing it for forty years.

Terry: Really. *Deep breath* What the hell is this? It's telephone lines. Okay. So, does someone either work in a utility company? Was there phone problems or this could be communication problems?

Deborah: It might be communication problems. We don't know anyone in the phone company or utilities.

Terry: Okay. Because the mothers are working together right now.

Deborah: Nice.

Terry: Okay. Because I'm asking. I said this makes no sense.

Cosmo: Oh no. I was going to say Joey ███████. The kid that passed in 2001. His father was the vice president of the telephone company.

Terry: Oh. There you go. And Joe's here. So you're going to hear from his dad. Do you normally talk to him?

Cosmo: I ran into him a couple of months ago. He still lives where he lives in Elmsford.

Terry: Okay. "So tell my dad I'm okay."

Cosmo: Really?

Terry: That's why. The communication. So he's having a hard time communicating with his father because the father maybe doesn't have the belief. So he came in first and made himself established because our mother said Joseph's here.

Cosmo: Yeah.

Terry: "Just tell my dad I'm okay. Stop worrying. I'm okay."

Cosmo: Alright.

Terry: Okay. Wow. He writes the initial "W". I don't want to go to Billy because we already went there.

Cosmo: Billy's first name was William.

Terry: They're saying no. This is another one. It could be another William, another Billy, Will, Willy.

Deborah: Here or there?

Terry: Living. Walter?

Cosmo: What about him?

Terry: I don't know. He just wrote the "W". Until I get an acknowledgement.

Cosmo: The only thing I can think of is the guy I work with is Billy.

Terry: What's his name?

Cosmo: Bill ███████.

Terry: Oh. He's another Bill.

Cosmo: Yeah. And he has a drinking problem.

Terry: Yes. He has a drinking problem.

Cosmo: And a drug problem.

Terry: There you go. He has to be careful.

Cosmo: Well, he had a heart scare, but he doesn't have insurance so they wouldn't take him. He had the same thing I had. What did I have?

Deborah: Atrial flutter.

Cosmo: Atrial flutter and he's not doing anything about it. Oh, he's eating garlic. He thinks that's going to solve the problem.

Terry: No. He can claim a charity case if he goes into the hospital.

Cosmo: Really.

Terry: Yeah. He can claim a charity case.

Deborah: You have to tell him that.

Cosmo: Even with the money he makes?

Terry: Oh, he makes fucking money. Why doesn't he have insurance?

Cosmo: Oh. This one's got a mouth on her. *Laughs*

Deborah: She calls it like she sees it.

Cosmo: Yeah, he has to make at least fifty grand a year.

Terry: You know what, just say it's charity.

Deborah: It couldn't hurt to say it.

Cosmo: Alright.

Terry: Go in through the emergency room. They discover heart. Say, "I have no money". I have to be a charity case," and they'll get him temporary medicaid for that. Okay?

Cosmo: I had a friend of mine that was a twin also. His name was Billy. He passed away.

Terry: No. I'm not there. *Points to the veil*

Cosmo: Okay. I didn't know what side you were going to do.

Terry: Yeah. Is it you with the feet problems?

Cosmo: You know, it's funny you should say that. My brother just had the gout the other day.

Terry: Okay. Because your mother is going to the foot.

Cosmo: Well, I have numbness in my legs from nerve damage.

Terry: Okay.

Cosmo: Just to let you know.

Terry: Okay. She's going more towards the feet. Or is someone prediabetic?

Deborah: Dawn is diabetic.

Terry: No. Not Dawn. *Points to Cosmo* It's your mother talking, so it would be your family she's talking about. Or does someone normally get swollen feet?

Cosmo: All I know is that my brother had the gout the other day.

Terry: Does that affect the foot?

Cosmo: Yeah. He had the gout in the foot.

Terry: Oh. There you go. So she's giving me a current event. They have to either give me current events or memories to stay with me. So she's saying she knows this. Did you ride horses? Who rode horses?

Cosmo: I was with horses yesterday.

Terry: There you go. So was your mother.

Cosmo: At the farm.

Deborah: See.

Terry: There you go.

Cosmo: Yeah. We pet them and everything.

Terry: So your mother is feeding the horses. So your mother was there with you, she's telling me.

Cosmo: Wow. She should be on the back of the truck helping me.

Deborah: *Laughs*

Cosmo: Put the hook on Ma. *Laughs*

Terry: Who's Vinny?

Cosmo: I have a cousin Vinny.

Terry: Okay. She went to visit Vinny.

Cosmo: Is he dead?

Terry: No.

Cosmo: Oh. This Vinny we haven't seen in like thirty years. He's our first cousin.

Terry: Okay. So it won't be a coincidence if you hear from him or about him. Again, they don't show me bad.

Cosmo: Oh. I'm sorry. Vinny, my cousin, just called me.

Terry: Oh. There you go. So your mother is giving me all current events.

Cosmo: I just got in touch with him after a long time. So when we did our vow renewal, we invited him.

Terry: Oh. Isn't that funny? So your mother, she knows this. She wants to give current events to you.

Cosmo: Ask her who's winning the super bowl this year.

Terry: Why is the dog making me feel his bark is better?

Cosmo: He had that raspy bark. Remember?

Deborah: He did.

Terry: He did. Oh. Okay. So it's better. It's fuller he's making me feel.

Cosmo: Good.

Deborah: Makes me feel better.

Terry: Who's taking his ashes?

Deborah: We have them.

Terry: I know, but who's taking them? Is it the first one that passes?

Cosmo: You mean between us? I would say either way, Mom would be.

Terry: Because he makes me feel his ashes are there, but they're not going to stay there because when one of you passes, it's going.

Cosmo: Oh no. We're transporting them out of one to another.

Terry: Oh, is that it?

Deborah: We just got a really nice urn.

Cosmo: An urn with a Pitbull head.

Deborah: Engraved.

Terry: Oh, so it was temporary.

Cosmo: We're switching them over.

Deborah: To a nicer urn.

Terry: Oh. There you go. So that's what he's showing me. So he's trying to prove that he's fine.

Cosmo: Good.

Terry: Okay. You still smell at night, though.

Cosmo: I smell?

Terry: Yeah. Do you burp or does he, um, smell when he sleeps? Because the dog is telling me, "He still smells at night".

Cosmo: *Laughing* I'm a garbage man.

Deborah: You do.

Cosmo: *Still laughing* That sucks.

Terry: Sorry, but the dog…

Cosmo: Bambino's complaining about me?

Deborah: *Cracking up* Oh my God.

Cosmo: Wait until I see him.

Deborah: You're not going to see him for a while.

Terry: Are you giving the surviving pit large bones to chew on?

Cosmo: Yeah.

Deborah: We were giving her his bones, but then we didn't realize, because they're both highly allergic dogs, that she was allergic, so we had to stop giving them to her.

Terry: Yes. I'm telling you the God's honest truth. This dog made me feel don't do that. Don't do that. She's going to get sick.

Deborah: And she did. She started scratching, and I looked at the thing, because these were his treats. She has her treats. And I said I want to start giving her Bambino's treats, and then she started scratching like crazy.

Terry: Yeah. No.

Deborah: Yeah. No. We stopped. We brought them back to the store.

Terry: Okay. Be careful with what you give her. It's so funny, this dog is talking to me.

Cosmo: Good.

Terry: Does she have any mouth problems? Teeth problems?

Deborah: They ground her teeth down. Before we got her, she was a bait dog.

Terry: Aw.

Deborah: So the long canines that are supposed to be sharp, but they're dull.

Cosmo: They grind them down and throw them in the pit to fight other dogs, but she doesn't have a chance because she can't grab. You know?

Deborah: She's beautiful though, otherwise.

Terry: Okay. Because he makes me feel, so this dog knows he also has to prove it's him. He can't just show up. Do you know what I mean?

Cosmo: He just went for surgery too. To the dentist. We sent him to have his teeth done.

Deborah: Bambino did.

Terry: Oh. So this is why he talks about this area as well. Was he the one that was limping? Or maybe he had his paw...

Deborah: His paw. He had this one paw. It was an allergy and it was all red.

Terry: He's telling me, "Everybody was looking here *Points to mouth*, but I had problems here." *Points to hand*

Cosmo: It was underneath.

Deborah: Because here was red. *Points to hand*

Terry: Yeah. It was, but there was something either in it or there was pain there too. But this, everyone knew this, but didn't know this.

Cosmo: Yeah. Yup.

Deborah: It's what we saw on him. It was red.

Terry: You know, the dog, do you let the surviving dog smell his ashes?

Deborah: Yes and she's afraid of it.

Terry: Is she?

Deborah: She won't go near it. I figured it would make her feel better. She was sniffing the spot the other day where he ended up going unconscious and I just let her sniff sniff sniff, but she won't go near his ashes.

Terry: Oh. Because it doesn't make sense to her that he's in that box or whatever it is that he's in now. It just doesn't make sense. She'll have a complete turn around because she is going to see him. He will come there.

Deborah: Good. Good. Good.

Terry: You may see her do this *shakes head back and forth* because he's going to bite on the ear, but like nibble, not bite her.

Cosmo: She does that to me. You don't think she does that now?

Deborah: I don't know. I never really…

Cosmo: When we let her out today, did you see what she was doing with her paw? To the head? She kept going like this.

Deborah: Oh yeah.

Cosmo: I never saw her do that before.

Terry: Because the dog is around. He's just trying to tell you, "These are going to be the signs that she's going to see me. She's going to see me and then she'll be fine one day". Who had the tube down their throat? I'm on the other side. I'm male, not female.

Cosmo: On the other side?

Terry: Yes. This means passed.

Cosmo: I don't know.

Terry: Did they try to save someone? I had to either intubate or something and there's an initial "D" around this person.

Cosmo: D?

Terry: Yeah. If they don't give me their name they're going to give me the name of someone living. Do you know a Danny, Daniel, Dennis? It's a "D" name.

Cosmo: Her son's name is Danny.

Deborah: Yeah, but Danny didn't get into…

Terry: No. No. If they don't give me their name they're going to tell me how they know you. One of Danny's friends. Did someone have to try to revive him? Did he have to have a tube put down his throat?

Deborah: Not as far as I know.

Terry: Okay. So keep that in mind also. And who's the left-handed person?

Deborah: My grandfather.

Cosmo: Oh, the other side you mean?

Terry: Yeah.

Cosmo: Why? Is he here?

Terry: Yeah.

Cosmo: Is he petting the dog?

Terry: Everyone together is with this dog, by the way.

Cosmo: I believe it.

Terry: Yeah. That dog is not alone at all.

Deborah: Thank you because you had to tell him.

Terry: That's fine. You can believe me or not, but this dog came in with pretty good confirmations that he knows what he's talking about: the teeth, the paw, that his bark is better.

Cosmo: Yeah.

Terry: So he's fine. Okay. So with this piece of paper, you have two choices. You can keep it or you discard it. The way to discard it: put it over the sink, put a match to it, let it burn just a little. As it burns just a little thank God for allowing, including the dog, everyone that came through.

Cosmo: Oh. We're not discarding it.

Terry: Okay.

Cosmo: We know that.

Terry: Oh. Okay. And then I promised God - you both have to do this - anyone I read I would ask them when they find themselves totally alone - so you can't be with each other - to say three informal prayers. Informal prayers sent by the heart. It's only a sentence or two. It's for three people living because *they* pray for us because we actually are closer to hell here. So it's for someone you care about, someone you don't even know because we have lost souls here, or someone you do know who is a lost soul and someone you don't like or trust. The prayer for that one goes something like - and your mother said, "Not my daughter". I don't know why she just said that.

Deborah: Not me?

Terry: No.

Deborah: Don't pray for Dawn?

Terry: Yeah. Dawn's not part of these prayers. Okay. The prayer for the person you don't trust or care for is, "You know what God, please let them find their way, but please keep them away from me". So wish them well, then create the boundary.

Cosmo: You'll explain that to me when we go home.

Deborah: *Laughs*

∞ The Story of Eight ∞

A Letter from Deborah

☆ ★ ☆ ★ ☆ ★ ☆ ★

We were thinking about the idea for about six months prior to when the final decision was made. As a family, we wanted to expand our inner circle from four to five. There were many questions that arose; money for one and could we open our hearts to another child in need? The answer was most definitely yes. Both my teenage sons, eighteen and fourteen at the time, were on board. So we pushed forward in our search.

When we first heard of our son, who was in foster care, we had to follow through immediately. We inquired with the agency and they sent us some pictures. Seeing those huge, kind eyes staring back at us tugged at our heartstrings immediately. We were told he was two years old and was a quiet, pensive soul who was always eager to please. We were hooked instantaneously. After some contact back and forth with the foster family, we were then put through a meticulous investigation including background and reference checks, along with multiple home visits and a neighborhood inspection. They wanted him to have the best home possible,

374

and we were more than willing to oblige with all of their requirements. That was how badly we wanted to bring this boy home. After all was said and done, thankfully, he became the fifth member of our brood and our family was complete.

Ten amazing years filled with laughter, love, and innumerable precious memories. Christmas cards with all my boys on the front were sent out every year. We enjoyed summer vacations as a family, holidays spent together, snuggles and endless hugs and kisses. Then came the day no one could ever prepare for. He was fine the night before, but I woke up to him vomiting. My oldest, Danny, heard him and immediately woke up my husband and I. Thinking he had a stomach bug, I cleaned him up and reassured him everything would be okay. However, as his mom, I knew something was wrong. It was something that came from being his mom, along with my innate intuition that told me this was not good. Unfortunately, the doctor's office was not open yet, so I tried to get him up so he could come on to our bed to rest and to comfort him. After a few unsteady steps, he collapsed onto the floor shaking, having what appeared to be a seizure, which was then followed by a stroke. He became unconscious. And it was then that I knew.

My husband and Danny thought he would regain consciousness, but something inside me told me they were wrong. Call it a mother's instinct if you wish, but I knew. I woke up my youngest, David, who was unaware of what had just transpired, and told him to say his goodbyes to our baby. We called the police for help to get him to the car so the doctor could see him. While we waited, we all took turns laying with him, telling him how much we loved him and how happy we were that he came into our lives. And although his eyes were closed, I knew he heard us.

When the officer arrived, he helped Danny and David carry him to our car. Though we drove there as fast as we could, tragically, he took his final breath on the ride to the doctor's office. To say we were devastated would be an understatement. The tears came and would not stop. The doctor said he must have had an underlying condition; something we could not have intercepted in time or predicted. Coming home to a "quiet" house was heartbreaking. There were no words to describe the overwhelming pain we felt as our family went from five to four in a heartbeat. This sweet, loving soul was such an important member of our family. His unconditional love was unending, and although there will always be a hole in our hearts from when he left us, we knew we gave him a home like no other. We loved him with all the love in our hearts and enjoyed our time with him every single day. A few weeks later, as we worked together to heal, my husband was told there was no such thing as an afterlife and that he would not be reunited with our son when he, himself, passed. After trying to explain to him that this was not true, I went for help to the only woman I knew who could fix this and ease his troubled heart. Yes, initially my husband was skeptical, even though I tried to convince him Theresa could help. However, after hearing through her reading that our baby was with us every day and yes, we would see him when our time on earth was over, he sighed with relief. The validations she gave him put his mind to rest and gave him closure, thankfully. Now, with the holidays here, we still cry, but not as much, and focus on remembering all the good times we had with our baby. We will always love him, the one who was affectionately known as the "sweetest Pitbull ever."

Shine on sweet Bambino, shine on.

★☆ The Medium ★☆ The Author ★☆ The Artist ★☆

TERRY MAROTTA is a Spiritual Medium for over six decades who has been able to recognize and communicate with those spirits and loved ones who have passed over. Her readings are saturated with the lightness that is God and His Angels. You can reach her at Terry.Marotta213@yahoo.com.

HEATHER STONE spent her life trying to fit into a world she didn't understand. She was once an odd child with an infatuation with the occult and all things otherworldly. And then she met Terry. That's when she learned what she thought was just an overactive imagination was really a third eye. She's spent the last few years studying Theresa's readings and learning her life story in order to bring you her last two books. A third book is in the works, and this time Terry has given Heather free rein. Guided by the spirit world, our third book will be an adventure in fiction based on Terry's real life readings and Heather's crazy idea of what life means - both in this world and the next. You can reach her at HeatherTCross@gmail.com.

MELISSA MULLAHEY is an NYC based artist working professionally for almost 30 years as a tattooist, painter and art instructor. She has art shows planned for 2023. You can reach her at MrsMullahey@gmail.com.

How to Reach Us

Check out our website by scanning this image with your phone's camera.

SCAN ME

Soulfulgatherings.net

If you haven't read our first book here's a little peek into what you missed.

Too Bad You're Going To Hell: A collection of stories and readings by Spiritual Medium Theresa Marotta Written by Heather T. Stone

Chapter 1

THE LADY IN WHITE

I grew up in the Bronx on Astor Avenue with my big, Roman Catholic, Italian family. My immediate family lived on the top floor of a two-family house owned by my Grandmother. She lived downstairs with two of her daughters - my Aunts. Grandma also owned the six family house on the same property. My Uncle had one of those apartments.

With everyone so close, my childhood playmates included five siblings and seven first cousins. We lived together, stayed together, and all us kids played together every day. Between our two buildings was a big yard where we got to hang out when it was nice out. It was a great setup. Life was good.

Our house was old. It had a full-length attic that ran the entire length of our apartment below, accessible through a full set of stairs off the Television Room. We called it the Television Room because that was the only thing in the room. Well, technically there was a bookcase too, but no couch or chairs or anything else.

Once the house fell asleep, Dad and I would curl up on the floor with a blanket and watch that television. We'd watch our favorite anchorman read the day's news reports and when it was over, we'd both fall asleep to a late-night movie. This was our routine. Just me and Dad - as soon as Mom and my little sister went to sleep. Well, at least it was like that at first. As time passed on, I had to wait for Mom and all five siblings to pass out before I got my alone time with Dad.

When I was three years old, I used to go upstairs and into the attic to play or ride a little red tricycle my Mom kept up there. The attic was the perfect place to ride it as it consisted of three rooms that connected to each other. One room was full of clothes being stored until the seasons changed - the type of clothes that cluttered up closets when the weather was warm. The middle room held lots of small knick-knacks and vintage kitchenware. Then there was a third and final room, but it wasn't on my route.

I loved that little red tricycle. I rode it all hours of the day; between the racks of sweaters and into the middle room, swing around the old typewriter, speed up near the pile of snow boots, hit a hard left and end up right where I started, which is precisely where I wanted to be so I could start again. It was so much fun. But, believe it or not, as fun as riding that little red tricycle was, it wasn't even the best part.

The most exciting part of my daily adventure was the anticipation of playing with my very own playmate, the Lady in White. I could always find her in the attic. She was a beautiful woman, about my mother's age. She had big brown eyes and the sweetest smile and always wore a long white dress. Not just any dress. It was always the same long, white dress. A gorgeous, long, white dress fit for a princess; the most remarkable dress my three-year-old eyes had ever seen. I loved the way it hung past her feet, making it seem as though she were floating. I never did learn her name, but it didn't matter. I referred to her as the Lady in White.

It's hard to explain how we met. It was almost as if she was always there since as far back as I was. My oldest memory of her was seeing her come out of the room that kept the out of season clothing. The out of season clothing room was full of those long types of stand-alone racks you see in retail shops today; each rack full. I'd go in there, start playing with my toys I kept there, and wait for her to appear.

The Lady in White was a kind woman who always had something nice to say. I couldn't tell you what her voice sounded like because we never used words to communicate. When we had something to tell each other we said it inside our heads - telepathically. She made me feel special; protected. I knew she loved me and I felt safe when she was around. She was a normal part of everyday life, for me, at least. See, back then I didn't realize no one else could see her, but that all changed the day my little sister got hurt under my watch.

One day my little sister - the only sibling I had so far - wanted to come up in the attic with me. I didn't want to bring her to my special place, but she cried until my mother told me I had to bring her with me. I trudged upstairs with her in tow and started to explain the rules. As soon as we were high enough to see over the crest of the stairs, she took one look at the tricycle and ran full speed towards it. She tried to climb up too quickly and fell - flat on her face, bumping her chin on the handlebar on the way down. Luckily, the Lady in White was already here.

"Go get Mommy," my sister wailed.

"It's okay," I told her. "The Lady in White is here. She can help you."

She looked at me, took a long breath and let out another cry. "Mommy!"

"Don't cry," I told her. "The Lady in White will help you".

I guess maybe she didn't like the Lady in White though I couldn't imagine why. The next thing I know she's climbing down the stairs, sobbing all the while. A few minutes later up comes Mom with that look on her face that said 'you're in big trouble little girl'.

"Theresa, why didn't you call me when your sister got hurt. You're the big sister. It's your job to watch over her."

"It's okay Mommy," I explained. "The Lady in White is here. She was watching over us."

"What do you mean the Lady in White is here?"

"She's right here." I pointed to her. She was standing in the corner next to a stack of boxes labeled "kitchen".

Mom looked confused. And still angry.

"The Lady in White is right here", I explained. "She was watching us, Mommy. I wasn't in charge."

My mother took a deep breath and walked downstairs without saying a word. A few minutes later she returned with a black-and-white photo I'd never seen before. She sat down in an old chair, held the photo out and asked a very simple question. "Do you see the Lady in White?"

There were several people in the photo, but I noticed her right away and shook my head yes.

Mom took another deep breath. "Can you point to the Lady in White?"

I shook my head again and lifted my finger to the Lady in White.

"Are you sure?"

Of course I was. What kind of question was that? The Lady in White was now standing right next to me. Couldn't she see for herself?

That's when I realized she couldn't. Mom couldn't see the Lady in White. Neither could my little sister. No one could.

Mom looked tongue-tied. She just stood up, walked back downstairs and never talked about it again. It didn't bother me in the slightest. I still wanted to spend my special time with the Lady in

White. I wasn't afraid of her even though no one could see her but me. It's hard to explain what it's like to grow up with a third eye because it's normal to you. The Lady in White was a part of my day-to-day life, just like my other spiritual guide and protector, the Blessed Mother that lived in my backyard.

The tricycle wasn't the only reason I liked being in the attic. Out of the attic window, you could see the statue of the Madonna standing on a snake in a concrete block. My Grandmother was devoted to our Lady and put that statue there the day she moved in. However, at the age of three, I had no concept of what religion was. I didn't know my Grandmother was devoted to the Blessed Mother, or that the statue was so old, put into place so long ago that the sun washed away all traces of its original coloring, leaving it a creamy white. It was because of Her coloring that I also referred to Her as the Lady in White. She was also my friend whom I talked to often.

I worried about Her sometimes, always standing on a snake. I asked Her if it hurt. She said it didn't. I asked Her why She stood on it and why it didn't hurt and why She always had "sparkles" fluttering around Her head.

"In time you'll know. In time you'll understand," was Her answer. "The timing isn't right for you now. Wait until you're older."

She was right. Back then I was too young to understand what was happening - why I could see and hear things other people couldn't. I was too young to understand why my mother never mentioned that day in the attic or the Lady in White ever again, but her actions were enough to warrant me never to bring it up either. I kept my secret gift to myself and continued to grow up intuitive, believing there was something wrong with me.

Made in the USA
Columbia, SC
19 February 2023

12557029R00245